Arms Against Faith

Arms Against Faith

How the U.S. Has Underestimated the Power of the Islamic World

By

Eladio Pasqual, Ph.D.

REGENT PRESS
OAKLAND, CALIFORNIA

ISBN: 1-58790-064-5

Library of Congress Control Number: 2004090116

First Edition

Manufactured in the U.S.A.

REGENT PRESS
6020-A Adeline Street
Oakland, CA 94608
regentpress@mindspring.com

I thank my wife and my two children for being tolerant while doing the research and writing this book for the last three years. I want to thank too, Steve, E.D. and Brian, the co-hosts of the Fox and Friends' program. They were a daily inspiration for three years, 1999 to 2003.

table of contents

one:

introduction

THE DESIRE TO BROADEN THE horizons of our two
children, twelve and thirteen years of age, was what brought
our family of four to Spain. Initially, it was a grand adventure –
sleek trains, famous cities, culture, history – for a while, traveling
was enjoyable. But the sight of yet another ancient castle, cathe-
dral, or palace made my youngsters restless. More castles? How
many cathedrals can there be? Our peripatetic life-style was no
longer exciting for them and we realized that our original idea
needed some fine tuning; it was time to settle down.

The children started complaining about missing their friends,
their school, and their home in the U.S. Their comments raised
concern, but it was not until they started at their new school that
truly dark clouds appeared on the horizon. The two youngsters
complained of isolation and discrimination. What had originally
been a minor problem was now a major worry.

For a while we hoped that the anti-American environment
would not affect them too much, but that hope vanished when

they became subject to name calling and other insults. To give them their due, my children have used the anti-American environment as an opportunity to reflect upon and feel proud of their heritage and their country, the U.S. They had been good about trying to learn from the experience they were going through. As their father, however, I found myself deeply troubled.

The anti-American "weed" grows ever more densely in fertile European soil. Born of a resentful "seed," it is fed every day with new and increasingly potent fertilizer. It has thrived on the compost of fault-finding and criticism mixed with exaggeration, magnification, pretentiousness, and a false sense of superiority on the part of European intellectuals, pundits, and politicians. The seed is planted and replanted daily in the European media.

The belief that anti-Americanism is a passing storm or a trend that will quietly fade away is an illusion. As much as Americans would like to deny it, those who live and work abroad are all to aware of this problem. One senior U.S. official involved in European relations was actually quoted in *The International Herald Tribune* as saying, "A lot of the world does not like America and it's going to take years to change their hearts and minds" (Becker & Dao, 2002, p. 3). Thinking that their hearts and minds can be changed at all, of course, is an the optimistic view of the situation. Anti-American sentiment in Europe is deep-rooted and complex; indeed, it is part of a world-wide phenomenon that is probably here to stay.

As I started work on this book, the Clinton administration was in its last days. It had been an era of political successes and personal scandals, but looking back now, the weaknesses that appeared so clearly in the Republican administration that followed were already visible.

Still, when Democrat Al Gore vied for election against Republican George W. Bush in 1999, European political leaders and analysts doggedly supported the democratic status quo rather than lean toward a party led by an adamant advocate of capital punishment. And when the final tally was questioned because of unreliable vote counting procedures, European critics seemed to actually enjoy pointing the finger at the culprits: corruption, decadence, nepotism. It was, after all, not every day that one got to accuse the last superpower – self-appointed beacon for democracy – of such behavior.

Time passed, but the criticism leveled at Mr. Bush did not lose its intensity. In fact, it flared up as he chose his cabinet and began to govern. The burial of the 1972 ABM treaty, the refusal to sign the Kyoto Protocol, and the plan to go through with the anti-missile project all demonstrate what political analysts Bumiller and Sanger (2002) called the president's "true stripes" (p. 4). Mr. Bush was labeled a unilateralist, uncooperative, uncommunicative, and arrogant.

It was in this anti-American atmosphere that the unthinkable happened. As the Twin Towers of the World Trade Center collapsed in the terrorist attacks of September Eleventh, the European critics and politicians saw a glimpse of the other side of Mr. Bush, namely his humanity. Suddenly, he was perceived as being humble and capable of asking for help, but this perception did not last long.

Thus, even as the demonstrations of empathy and solidarity with the American people continued, the political analysts took up their battle positions once more and began to speculate on what the U.S. government, led mostly by the Pentagon at this point, would do now. They feared that the guiding forces of U.S. policy after the attacks would be the spirit of vengeance, the will for retaliation, and the punishment of those involved, even at the expense of innocent lives. Europeans, after having dealt with the terrorist threat in their own countries for years, felt like the U.S. was acting viscerally after having turned a blind eye for so long.

The fact is that for decades the U.S. had been overly tolerant of terrorism, allowing fund raising activities for the IRA and providing political haven for numerous individuals pursued by their own countries for their terrorist actions. More recently, after attacks on its citizens and property in countries like Kenya, Tanzania, and Yemen, the U.S. Government had become more vocal against terrorism, but still in a very lenient, almost passive way. Then one morning, the U.S. awoke to awful television images of a full-scale terrorist attack within its own borders. It was only after the September Eleventh attacks that the U.S. decided that it must take urgent measures to protect its citizens from this deadly threat.

Such was the impact of the attacks that the U.S. decided to take unilateral military action, thereby avoiding time-consuming planning and complicated arrangements with its allies. Time was considered to be of the essence and the government wanted to take urgent action.

This determination to go it alone was described by European politicians and analysts as adventurous, dangerous, and even pretentious. While some see the U.S. heading for a potential repeat of the Vietnam War, others insist we are there now. As Paul Steiger (2001) wrote in the European edition of *The Wall Street Journal*, "The United States is not headed into a quagmire; it is already in one." Steiger goes even further, using the Russians' experience in Afghanistan to assert that "President Bush is facing the most brutish, corrupt, wily and patient warriors in the world, nicknamed dukhi or ghosts by flayed Russian soldiers who saw them melt away" (p. 4).

While it has been easy for Europe to criticize America in its "War against Terrorism," it smacks of cynicism. The European governments themselves have consciously disregarded the complexities and ignored the international repercussions of the problem that has been brewing for over a decade in Afghanistan, ever since its child warriors, the Mujahidin, along with Al Qaeda, or Islamic Volunteers, routed the Russian army.

In contrast to the passivity of the U.S. and Europe, several Middle Eastern countries, most notably Pakistan and Saudi Arabia, did not ignore what was happening in Afghanistan. Long before the terrorist attacks on the World Trade Center, both countries set out to achieve their different objectives; Pakistan, through its secret police, helped shape and influence the Taliban, whereas Saudi Arabia used its financial power to manipulate and indoctrinate Afghani refugees in fundamentalist beliefs.

During the entire lead-up to September Eleventh, the U.S. maintained its tolerant position with regard to the Taliban; that is until they were confronted with terrorism on an unprecedented scale in their own country.

The events seem clear-cut, but they are rooted in an extremely complex context. It is my aim to provide some insight into this context, so as to give the reader some perspective and awareness of the main issues which affect the Middle East and the world as a whole today.

Thus, my first task will be to offer an account of the human response to the tragedy of September Eleventh in New York, Washington, and Pittsburgh, in order to get a better perspective on the psychological consequences and the political ramifications that have been brought about by the attacks. These topics will occupy Chapters 2 and 3 of this book.

Chapter 4 will delve into the manner in which the U.S. government was forced to reassess national security and the safety of its citizens, who for their part demanded more information about the perpetrators and called for them to be brought to justice.

The topic of terrorism itself, in all its aspects, will be the subject of Chapter 5, while Chapter 6 will examine the panic set off by terrorism and the psychological urge to fight it with all possible means.

Chapter 7 will deal especially with Al Qaeda, the terrorist group protected and fomented by the Taliban and the Afghan army, and which was responsible for the September Eleventh attacks.

Because religion is a major motivating factor for this new breed of terrorists, Chapter 8 will examine how Islam, the world religion followed by over a billion people, is misquoted and misused by the fundamentalist militants to promote terrorist activities.

Al Qaeda's plans for gaining access to nuclear weapons will be examined in Chapter 9. These plans have been pieced together from files left behind as the members of the terrorist group fled Afghanistan for safe havens, oftentimes in European countries. Indeed, as anti-terrorist action has gained momentum in Europe, more of these plans have been verified.

Al Qaeda's purpose is ostensibly to aid the Palestinian cause; thus, any plans the organization may have to amass sophisticated arms is a direct concern for the state of Israel, which uncomfortably shares a roof with the fledgling Palestinian state. The special concerns of Israel will be discussed in Chapter 10.

Chapter 11 will examine how American foreign policy has elicited contradictory views of the U.S., while Chapter 12 will discuss the way in which this has in turn triggered criticism, resentment, and increasing anti-Americanism. Chapter 13 reviews the relationship between the U.S. and the European Union (E.U.) as well as the changes recent events have wrought on the North Atlantic Treaty Organization (NATO). The changing role of the U.N. and its security council will be discussed in Chapter 14. Chapter 15 will examine the rise of the new "Super Power" of public opinion during the crises that preceded the war in Iraq, which will be discussed in Chapter 17. The phenomenon of globalization and its dark side will be covered in Chapter 16. Chapter 18 contains an overview of President Bush. Finally, the epilogue will dare to take a glimpse at some of the worst case scenarios, which will hopefully never occur.

two:
september eleventh,
2001

BEFORE GOING ANY further, the thousands of victims of the terrorist attacks on September Eleventh deserve special mention and remembrance because
They have died
In the radiant sunrise of the world.
They have died
When the world was beginning its dawn.
They have died
Among their own and for their own;
Thank you for such tireless generosity.
For those of us who watched the events of September Eleventh from afar there was no time for sophisticated explanations or observations because the obvious spoke so plainly. Silence, reflection, and prayer filled our house and many other homes around the world.

The television kept our eyes focused on horrific images of despair and bravery, pictures of a person desperately seeking help by waving a white cloth from a window of the World Trade Center, images of the courageous man who jumped from one of the upper floors of one of the towers; all these appeared again and again throughout that day and those that followed, not letting anyone miss the terror.

News stories repeatedly reminded viewers of all those who had died both inside the Twin Towers and in the immediate surroundings: the civilians who had arrived to work slightly earlier that day, the police officers and fire fighters who had rushed to the scene to assist the victims as the first tower caught fire, all those who were trapped in the buildings and then under the fallen rubble as the towers collapsed.

Our minds were flooded with fear and also with awe at the sheer level of destruction. There were so many questions without answers that day.

After the initial shock, many people wanted to hide by turning off their televisions and averting their eyes from the scenes of panic showing immense crowds covered with dust, fleeing from the area of the Ground Zero. Although there were two other "plane bombings", one at the Pentagon and another which failed its target and crashed near Pittsburgh, the attack on New York was what caught everyone's attention.

It was not merely the sheer magnitude of the bombing, which brought down two of the tallest buildings in the world and left over 3000 people dead, that made the New York attack the most compelling. It was the fact that the Twin Towers, symbols of U.S. prosperity, located in the middle of America's most paradigmatic city, had suddenly been turned into a mausoleum for thousands of innocent people. The attack on the World Trade Center will thus be remembered by every American as the definitive symbol in the War on Terror.

Watching the footage over and over again, apart from trying to ascertain who the perpetrators were and what their motive could possibly be, the other question that kept running through everyone's mind was: who were the innocent victims?

The answer is simple. The victims were mostly Americans, New Yorkers. But this simple answer covers a diversity hard to come by anywhere else, for these victims were White, Hispanic, Asian, African-American, Protestant, Catholic, Jewish, Muslim, people from both the Northern and Southern Hemispheres, people of every race, creed, and color. These were the victims of what the news quickly dubbed the "Attack on America."

The U.S. has long been and continues to be the paradigm of a multicultural, multiracial society. Even with its problems, it is seen as a shining example to many people all over the world and as such, this original, progressive, and dynamic idea of an integrated society has often been the subject of praise by many European analysts who would like to see this human phenomenon become a model for all civilized countries. By the same token, however, many international critics, nurtured by an active anti-American sentiment, saw the terrorist attacks of September Eleventh as a consequence of what they consider to be unenlightened American policies around the world.

To understand the impact of September Eleventh, one has to understand the general American psyche. Such a generalization must perforce be painted with an extremely broad brush, but on the whole it is safe to say that the majority of U.S. citizens are proud to be Americans in good times and bad. They love their country and regard it as something akin to a shining fortress. Most enjoy lives of freedom and prosperity and most are content with their country's economic and technological prowess.

Most Americans consider themselves to be patriotic, which they see as a positive trait. This does not rule out, however, the willingness to criticize their own government. As author and journalist Noah Gordon (2002) wrote, "As a citizen of a democracy, I am able to express a respectful discrepancy regarding how my government acts militarily and diplomatically" (p. 6). Like Gordon, many Americans censure the political or military decisions of their leaders, yet when they feel that the armed forces are needed to protect the U.S. Constitution and everything it stands for, Americans tend to come together to support their government.

The outside world often misinterprets American casualness, lack of sophistication, and naiveté for arrogance, self-importance, and obnoxiousness. Americans are often seen as being spoiled and poor losers, but in many instances, their behavior is due to the fact that they do not like to be threatened. Thus, when they feel menaced by an enemy, the Americans tend to put aside their differences of race, color, and creed to unite behind their leaders.

September Eleventh galvanized the Americans in just such a fashion. The attacks have made both politicians and the public in general more cautious, concerned, even suspicious. U.S. citizens have come to realize that the liberal society they have enjoyed for decades is precisely what allowed weaknesses to creep into specific sectors such as immigration control and airline safety. Indeed, many factors contributed to making things easy for those with evil intentions.

Surprisingly, one of these factors may actually be the dynamic pace of life in the U.S., which tends to keep people preoccupied with their own lives, jobs, and tasks. Many, if not most, choose to leave public concerns to public policy makers, relying on their elected officials to take full responsibility for them in matters of security and vigilance. In addition, this focus on their own lives often leads average U.S. citizens to ignore the pain and misery in the world around them. This ability to overlook the hungry and poor of the world has been a noticeable characteristic of the U.S. government and its policies.

The terrorist attacks of September Eleventh mark the beginning of a new chapter in the history of the U.S. and its people. Americans now know that it is time to take a better look at the interests and influence of the U.S. beyond its national borders. One thoughtful American commented after the attacks, "I hope my children don't grow up as isolated as I did. I expect that they will appreciate their country more and have more understanding of international issues" (cited in Lloris, 2001, p. 2). In short, Americans must stop judging everyone and everything solely from a U.S. perspective.

Obviously, September Eleventh has changed how Americans view the world, but it has also changed how the world sees Americans, for the event showed the individual, human side of America. Americans were suddenly seen as people who experience pain and fear, and who can be made to feel vulnerable. American patriotism was seen from a different angle, as that of a people united by their common principles and values to resist adversity. And perhaps precisely because this human side of America has been laid so open, the rest of the world can now make its needs known to the last superpower.

The poor of the world want America to know that they too want to be part of tomorrow. Television cameras tend not to focus on the poor, but these people now feel that they can get America's attention while the Americans are still alert. They want Americans and their leaders to know that millions of people around the world live with less than one dollar a day and that half of the world's working population earns less than two dollars a day. They want Americans to know that millions go to bed hungry and that one quarter of the world's population has never tasted a glass of suitable drinking water. That every minute one woman in the world dies in childbirth. They want the U.S. to be aware of the monumental tragedy that AIDS is causing in the developing world, where 23 million people die every year because of this disease. Without prevention and education, there will be 100 million HIV carriers in the next five years.

But AIDS is just one of the scourges of the developing world, along with malaria, tuberculosis, and dysentery. One out of four people in the world will die of one of these diseases; the majority will be children without access to safe drinking water.

The world population will double in the next fifty years. This increase will occur disproportionately in the poorest nations, which have no financial or economic means to support this growth. They want and desperately need the wealthier nations, lead by the U.S., to help them tackle the problems of poverty, hunger, and disease. Americans are a generous people, but ironically, official U.S. policy has long ignored the plight of the developing world. The terrorist attacks on the Twin Towers may change this tendency. As Thomas Friedman, a columnist for the New York Times wrote, "If anything has been learned from September Eleventh, 2001, it is that if you don't visit a bad neighborhood, it will visit you" (cited in Johnston, 2001, p. 6).

three:
did anything
really happen?

September eleventh didn't have the apocalyptic consequences
some might have imagined. It turned out that the United
States wasn't as weak and isolated as he [bin Laden] thought.
— David Ignatius (2001, p. 6)

VULNERABILITY

SUICIDE TERROR IS MEANT TO cause death and destruction in the most spectacular way possible; its purpose is to
leave innocent people feeling intensely vulnerable by making their
surroundings seem breached and unsafe.

Ironically, the survivors of the Twin Towers used this sense of
vulnerability to empower themselves and help one another. As Jim
Dwyer (2002) of The New York Times noted, "Even when the situation was most hopeless, the trapped people were still watching out
for one another" (Final moments..., p. 2).

Even though most Americans have been exposed to danger and misfortune at one time or another, European critics and analysts dwelt on the subject of this "new" vulnerability for weeks, as if to drive home to citizens of the U.S. that they were not invincible. Indeed, Americans took this warning to heart. For years, the U.S. has been thought of as one of the safest places on earth, a "fortress," as one analyst wrote. Although the U.S. took part in many armed conflicts during the 20th Century, the closest any enemy came to them was in the bombing of Pearl Harbor. But September Eleventh exposed unprotected fissures. Americans realized that the personal freedoms they enjoy had allowed the enemy to work from within.

This observation, in turn, humbled many Americans, or at least gave them a new empathy for people of other nations in similar situations. As David Ignatius (2001) commented, "It is good that Americans now know what it is like to be vulnerable. But that finding also suggests a sense of common humanity – a recognition that after September Eleventh we are truly all in the same boat" (p. 6).

Some critics exploited this theme of new-found American vulnerability to blame U.S. policies for much of the poverty and misery in the developing world. Other analysts took the opportunity to show their empathy and solidarity with the American people in these sensitive circumstances. International political observer Riad Z. Abdelkarim (2001) wrote:

> When the dust settles down within the carnage of New York and Washington and the names of the numerous victims are revealed, it will be evident that every faith, every ethnic group, and every race was a victim of this terror act... The victims will reflect the diversity of the country, one of the most noticeable strong points of the nation. (p. 24)

The Americans felt vulnerable, but the people made their vulnerability a source of strength and solidarity.

Nowhere was this more obvious than the hundreds of stories concerning the response of the firefighters at the scene of the horror. Months after the attack, a tape recording of "lost voices" that had been ignored by investigators showed that firefighters had actually reached the 78th floor of the South Tower when previous reports had stated that they had merely reached the 50th. Not only did they go further up the tower, the tape revealed that they had actually started to plan how best to extinguish the blaze and help the victims (Dwyer, 2002, Una cinta…, p. 18).

Another story relates how a window-washer saved the lives of six people with his cleaning brush. One of the survivors called the window-washer their "guardian angel" (Dwyer, 2002, Una cinta…, p. 18).

Still, the occasion has given rise to comments and reflections on how the Americans can use the vulnerability made manifest by September Eleventh to change and grow. Many have called for stricter regulations, some have even called for a new era of isolationism. Others want to promote just the opposite. Among the latter, the Chilean novelist Ariel Dorfman (2001), writing in the Spanish newspaper El País, comments that the U.S. must return the solidarity they were shown immediately after the crisis:

> The world reacted unanimously to the U.S. tragedy by showing solidarity and offering assistance. It remains to be seen whether the North American women and men molded by pain and resurrection will reciprocate by participating in the hard process of healing the wounded human race. (p. 30)

Dorfman hopes that the death and destruction experienced by the American people on September Eleventh serve the higher purpose of reminding all of the hunger and anguish many impoverished people endure all over the world.

The phenomenon of globalization and its dark side will be covered in Chapter 16.

SECURITY

A FTER THE ATTACKS, SEVERAL newspapers ran headlines indicating that Americans had lost faith in that best, and often most overlooked, of gifts: security.

The problem in a democracy that values personal freedom and individual rights is that absolute safety can never be guaranteed. Americans are aware of this and do not want to sacrifice their freedom to such a great extent. Rather, they feel that their main enemy and that of their democracy, namely terrorism, can only be defeated from a position of strength that does not compromise the values of freedom that America stands for.

Still, public safety has become a top priority for the Bush Administration. President Bush has said that the U.S. is not going to cross its arms and wait for another apocalyptic terrorist attack captained by any Osama bin Laden. Indeed, Bush is confident that all terrorist organizations are susceptible to weakness, just as the governments that support and protect them are. The war on terrorism has thus been declared and President Bush has vowed that terrorists and their supporters will be confronted with intelligence and resolution.

On a national level, then, the U.S. is determined and ready to engage in this ongoing struggle. On a more personal, individual level, however, the death and destruction of September Eleventh has made many Americans scared and confused.

An educator from New York put it this way: "I am a teacher; I am expected to solve the problems of my pupils. After all this, I do not know what to do" (cited in Marin, 2001, p. 14). Another American, a homemaker, expressed her confusion saying, "My husband and I are totally lost; we have a child and I don't know how to answer his questions" (cited in Marin, p. 14). The attacks have left the American people feeling suspicious and fearful of an enemy who moves among them, invisible and devious. Indeed, the thought of having a neighbor who seems totally ordinary go to a local church to get an assignment for carrying out a terrorist attack is unnerving and eerie precisely because it is now entirely plausible.

This feeling of fear and suspicion brought on by the attacks on September Eleventh were only heightened a few months later by the appearance of anthrax, a deadly bacterium. Several people in New York, Washington, and other cities became ill with anthrax and one employee at American Media in Boca Raton died as a result of inhaling the bacterium. While the origin of the outbreak is still undetermined, the threat of bioterrorism is obviously on everyone's mind, causing even more worry and concern. As Attorney General John Ashcroft said, "The danger of an attack with chemical or biological arms is real" (cited in: Washington, 2001, p. 11).

PROTECTION

THE ANALYSTS KNOW THAT NO COUNTRY, even the colossal U.S., can boast of total protection for its citizens. In fact, a free society with such an expansive territory is impossible to seal off and keep safe. Still, European critics had a hey-day picking apart the CIA and the FBI for their incompetence at keeping terrorists off of American soil, blaming Congress for weakening both agencies by cutting their funding.

Whatever the reasons behind the failure of the CIA and the FBI to keep Americans safe, the real question for the press was whether the American people could forgive the government agencies for their mistakes. Writing in the Spanish newspaper El País, Frances Stoner Sounders (2001) asserted that "The American people, dead and alive, have paid a high price for the secret [the security agencies] pay with their salaries" (p. 5). She further accused the FBI of ignoring clues which pointed directly to September Eleventh and doing nothing about individuals with possible terrorist connections. In fact, as early as 1999, two of the hijackers in the attacks were mentioned in a CIA bulletin as having connections to Osama bin Laden, being resident in the U.S, and planning an imminent terrorist attack; still, no action was taken against them.

The CIA was obviously tracking their movements, however, for on January 15, 2001, the agency noted that the two suspected terrorists flew from Bangkok to Los Angeles. Since the CIA never informed the Immigration and Naturalization Service of the two men's possible connections to an international terrorist organization, they entered the country with proper visas and no problems.

Furthermore, the two men continued to reside in the U.S. and maintain contacts with those who would become their fellow hijackers on September Eleventh. No move was made to detain or question them in any way. When this knowledge was made public after the attacks, it naturally raised a flood of questions about the power of the U.S. and its ability to protect itself. Over and over again people asked what exactly the FBI and the CIA had done with the information provided by their colleagues in the field.

Ironically, while the competence of the security agencies had been overestimated, the ability of the U.S. military to launch an attack on the Taliban in Afghanistan was obviously underestimated. In fact, most analysts were shocked at how badly they had miscalculated the readiness of the U.S. military, conceding that they had clearly misjudged the morale, capability, and power of the United States. Commenting on the success of the U.S. armed forces, Ralph Peters (2002), author and retired military officer, wrote, "The U.S. military embarked on an extraordinarily impressive program of learning-by-doing in wartime" (p. A10). As for the pessimism of the analysts, Peters wryly noted, "Fortunately, our military forces have done a grand job this time around of frustrating those who delight in American setbacks" (p. A10). Another commentator, the Polish historian Ryszard Kapuscinski (2002), shared his observations about the American people and their probable response to the tragedy of September Eleventh:

> The United States is a fortunate nation. It does not allow the past to cloud its mind and imagination. The U.S. mentality is open to the future.
>
> By being young, it is able to be creative without letting the past hold it back by binding its hands and feet. (p. 18)

LOSS OF CIVIL LIBERTIES?

AFTER THE TERRORIST ATTACKS, the government took measures designed to minimize the possibility of further terrorist action on U.S. soil. European critics were quick to characterize these measures as repressive, commenting that they would lead to a loss of rights and a deterioration of democracy. The main focus of this criticism centered around the loss of civil liberties from the abolition of secrecy, the unconditional detention of suspicious individuals, and the withholding of information to the public.

Later, a second wave of criticism was generated by the release of Vice-President Cheney's "Enduring Freedom" document. At a press conference, Cheney defended the policies outlined in the document, including the following:

• Undocumented individuals involved in terrorist activities will not have the right to be represented by an attorney as a legal resident or U.S. citizen would have.

• Individuals fleeing from their native countries and whose "report card" includes any activities which border on terrorist acts may be denied their request for asylum.

• The adoption and legitimizing of political assassination as an operative means by the U.S. military.

• The release of knowingly false information to the public.

Mr. Cheney's statements defending this document were labeled racist, discriminatory, and unfair.

Public outcry against possible losses of civil liberties did produce some changes to the document. Gabriel Jackson (2002), an American historian and sharp critic of the Bush administration, points out that the judiciary branch made several changes to the usually off-limits area of military tribunals in response to criticism from conservatives in the judiciary system. Two of the most salient changes are that suspects will always have the right to be represented by an attorney and that the media will be allowed to witness the judicial proceedings. Even with these modifications, however, Jackson asserts that the idea of legal process in the military tribunals is a farce. For one thing, during the trial itself, the Secretary of Defense or the presiding judge may reveal classified information not previously available to the defense. In addition, even if a suspect is found innocent, he may still be held without option for release if the court considers him to be potentially dangerous.

Needless to say, the legal repercussions of September Eleventh are still being hotly debated.

COULD IT HAPPEN AGAIN?

B RUCE HOFFMAN (2002), AN expert on terrorism gives the frighteningly simple answer: "Of course." The reasons, as expounded by Hoffman, are clear. One of the lessons of September Eleventh is that "Terrorists live to identify the vulnerable points and use them accordingly. There will always be breaches in any defense system. Total invulnerability is impossible" (p. 20). Hoffman thus echoes Thomas Jefferson's own observation that, "The price of freedom is eternal vigilance."

JUST IN CASE...

THE SEPTEMBER ELEVENTH ATTACKS have put Americans on their guard, and yet most people living in the U.S. have never sat down and made a concrete plan of action for the case of a terrorist attack. If you do not have such a plan, make one so that you and your family will be less likely to become confused, lost, and trying in vain to reach one another in the middle of a panicked city when disaster strikes.

four:
who are these people?

There are too many young people in the world who feel that their lives are worth nothing, ready to be utilized and give themselves the pleasure of destroying the world in front of the television cameras. Maybe it is the only pleasure left to them.
— Xavier Ruber de Ventos (cited in: Carlin, 2001, End of an era, p. 13)

WHEN FRENCH PHILOSOPHER CLAUDE Lefort (2001) was asked about the terrorists of September Eleventh, he responded that they were "God crazy militants" and that they were "well organized... people capable of living a normal modern life, unwilling to die without a cause and at the same time capable of making a religious sacrificial act," that is, by killing innocent people (p. 6).

If nothing else, the terrorist hijackers were extremely well prepared. For one, they were trained to outsmart airport security systems. They carried no guns or metal objects, but rather simple plastic knives and shavers, innocent common objects found in luggage and on airplanes as ordinary utensils. They were well-trained in the best way to overpower and replace the crew, cut communication with the control towers, and guide the airplanes to where they would cause maximum damage to the Twin Towers. The attacks were not careless schemes; they were carefully and patiently thought-out and executed.

But who would ever do such a thing? The hijackers themselves, most of whom (fifteen of nineteen) were from Saudi Arabia, were indoctrinated by "radical preachers" who filled their heads and hearts with anger towards the United States. As secret members of the radical terrorist group headed by Osama bin Laden, Al Qaeda, they went to live in the U.S. as students and businessmen. In fact, it is well documented how the hijackers were aided and abetted by over two hundred individuals affiliated with Al Qaeda in the U.S. and by hundreds more in Spain, England, France, Germany, and other European countries. What is not clear, though, is why anyone would actually go through with such a suicide attack. As Oxford historian Timothy Garton Ash (2001) remarked:

> What I have not seen yet in the tons of written essays is one that explains what is in the mind of a young man from Saudi Arabia who studies in Hamburg, Germany, travels through the U.S., lives in Ohio, hijacks an airplane and crashes it against the Twin Towers. Nobody has been able to explain it, maybe because it is too dangerous to get inside. (p. 21)

Perhaps, as Garton Ash points out, it is not a question to be answered with logic.

Initially, analysts thought that the September Eleventh attacks on New York, Washington, and Pittsburgh were too extensive and sophisticated to have been masterminded by bin Laden alone without the support of Afghanistan, which at the time was ruled by the Taliban government. This original assessment was then expanded as the experts contended that Afghanistan was too distant and isolated to initiate, plan, and lead such a complicated operation. Nevertheless, the terrorists, with their fanatical convictions, iron discipline, and incredibly complex network around the world, managed to stymie all the analysts.

Of course, they were helped by what was increasingly seen as the incompetence and unpreparedness of the U.S. government agencies. This opinion grew even stronger as people started to understand the magnitude of the attack: how could an operation demanding so much time, months of preparation, and training be carried out without being observed and stopped by the U.S. intelligence services, which include the FBI (Federal Bureau of Investigation), the CIA (Central Intelligence Agency), the NSA (National Security Agency), and the NRO (National Recognizance Office)?

Incredibly, the FBI did have information about the possibility of this type of attack, but it was ignored. One month before the attack, a flight instructor reported an individual for discussing the possibility of using a 747 jet loaded with fuel as an incendiary bomb. At the time, the individual in question, Zacarias Mousaoui, was arrested for immigration violations, but it was not until after the September Eleventh attacks that the FBI actually searched his home and belongings. Here they found a computer disk with information about using a plane to spread toxic chemicals over an urban area. The contents were similar to those found in the computer of Mohammed Atta, one of the hijackers in the September Eleventh attacks.

For their part, the CIA repeatedly ignored the threat posed by Al Qaeda to the U.S., its citizens, and its property overseas. For many people, September Eleventh, 2001 was the first time they had reason to note the name of the terrorist group, but its history of violent terrorist actions against America actually began in February 1993, when bin Laden carried out a car bomb attack in the underground parking lot of the World Trade Center in New York.

That attack left six dead and a thousand wounded. In November 1995, Al Qaeda was responsible for another car bomb which exploded in a college located in Riyadh, Saudi Arabia, killing five American teachers. In June 1996, a barracks at the American airbase King Abdul Aziz in Saudi Arabia was bombed; nineteen American airmen died as a result. In October 2000, Al Qaeda suicide terrorists crashed a boat bomb against the destroyer, USS Cole, leaving nineteen navy personnel dead.

Before September Eleventh, however, the most devastating attack by far was the simultaneous car bombing of the U.S. embassies in Nairobi, Kenya, and Dar-es-Salaam, Tanzania. Al Qaeda terrorists were once again responsible for the 270 dead, many of whom were not even directly affiliated with the embassies or the U.S.

In spite of these continuous, even large-scale terrorist attacks, no direct action was taken against Al Qaeda or their support groups in the U.S. and Europe. Indeed, they continued working avidly to prepare the apocalyptic attacks on New York, Washington, and Pittsburgh. What were the intelligence services doing all this time?

Harsh as it may seem, many insiders have accused these government agencies of becoming "soft," maintaining that the intelligence service agents prefer to live comfortably in the suburbs of Virginia rather than chase Islamic terrorists through the fifty states and overseas in Europe. In fact, most observers find it incredible that the CIA "does not have a single truly qualified Arabic-speaking officer" (Marozzi, 2001, p. 5). Thus, one of Al Qaeda's biggest aids was the situation within the CIA. It is also clear, however, that the terrorists were helped enormously by the philosophy of the new economy: the deadly trio of privatization, liberalization, and deregulation.

By privatizing airport security, the U.S. basically set up a potential breach of security which allowed the terrorists to carry out their plans with no obstacles. An official from the National Transportation Safety Board asserted, "The fact that the terrorists could get control of four airplanes in such a short time says everything." He further commented, "When a minimum salary is being paid, you get people of minimum wage" (cited in De Rituerto, 2001, p. 9). Incredibly, most airport security agents receive only a few hours of training and are hired with temporary contracts to avoid paying them benefits. And flight personnel receive even less training in such matters. As one pilot told a reporter, "We are trained to deal with trouble makers ... not with suicide hijackers" (cited in: De Rituerto, 2001, p. 9).

In addition, the steady liberalization of immigration laws and customs regulations opened the doors for the hijackers and their supporters. During the Clinton Administration, borders between the U.S. and both Canada and Mexico were deregulated and liberalized. Currently, 350,000 cars and 30,000 trucks go through customs daily along the 7,000 miles of border between the U.S. and its neighbors. The less restrictive laws made it much easier for members of Al Qaeda to enter the U.S. illegally and travel freely without any problems. When asked about the current threats to the U.S., many feel that liberalization has been the damnation of America.

At the center of the Al Qaeda web of terrorists and their supporters sits Osama bin Laden, founder and leader of the terrorist organization. He financed the September Eleventh attacks by funneling the money to the terrorist militants who took part. Unfortunately, money for such actions is not hard to come by; for years, fund raising by various extremist Islamic organizations has been the financial backbone of Al Qaeda, as well as other fundamentalist Islamic terrorist groups.

five:
terrorism

DURING THE REAGAN ERA, ALTHOUGH terrorism was a concern for the administration, it never came close to being a top priority. In the 1990s, terrorism was still a third-tier issue for those policy makers deciding matters of national security.

This attitude is all the more difficult to understand when one considers that in the two last decades of the twentieth century, 871 Americans died as a result of terrorist attacks on American facilities outside of the territorial U.S. Apparently, this figure did not seem significant to the high-ranking official who, at a meeting of the CIA counter-terrorism center, was quoted as saying that "Fewer Americans died from terrorism than drowned in bathtubs." (Barton, 2001, p.3).

It is easy to forget that terrorism was a threat long before the first attack on the World Trade Center in 1993. Previous to that date, the balance included the attack on the marine barracks in Beirut as well as an attack on the U.S. embassy in that same troubled city, numerous hijackings, the incident on the Achille Lauro, and the explosion of Pan Am flight 103. But it was not until the Clinton administration that the government made any systematic effort to fight terrorism in terms of allocating resources to anti-terrorist intelligence and activity. In a speech at Washington University in August of 1995, Clinton himself dubbed terrorism "the enemy of our generation," and called on the American people to prevail over this threat to the nation. Still, terrorism never became the Clinton Administration's top priority.

All this changed with the terrorist attacks on September eleventh, 2001. The present administration regards terrorism as one of its top priority issues and it will remain so in the foreseeable future.

But what exactly is terrorism anyway?

Back in the 80s, it was described as a "plague" and a "cancer spread by barbarians against civilization" (Chomsky, 2001, p. 3).

This definition is perhaps too literary, too vague, and too harsh to be of much use in diplomatic circles; however, those circles have yet to come up with a better description of the phenomenon. The United Nations Security Council, although it unanimously approved a resolution condemning terrorism, has yet to define what it means by the term. In fact, the concept has become a sort of insult to be hurled about by critics when they disagree with military or police action of any kind. Thus, various countries have been branded as terrorists, carrying out terror attacks on innocent victims.

The European Union, many of whose member states have had recurring terror attacks on their own soil, has endorsed a definition of terrorism formulated by six of its members, namely France, Spain, Germany, Portugal, Italy, and the United Kingdom:

> Terrorist acts are those intentionally perpetrated acts that can seriously hurt a country or an international organization when the acts are committed with the objective to gravely intimidate a population or to force public officials or international organizations to do or

stop doing a determined act, or to break down or destroy political, constitutional, economical and social structures of a nation or an international organization. (Cited in: A common language ..., 2001, p. 18)

Along with this goes the E.U. definition of a terrorist group as a "structural association of two or more people that acts in an arranged manner to commit terrorist acts" (A common language...). If these definitions have been agreed upon by the fifteen member states of the E.U. after the diplomats and statesmen have hammered them out with all the tact and skill they could muster, then they have withstood a very difficult test indeed.

For their part, Muslim scholars, gathered for six days in the holy city of Mecca in Saudi Arabia, developed their own definition of terrorism to be applied in the Islamic world. As Mr. Abdullah al Turki, General Secretary for the Arab League and spokesman for the group, pointed out, the working out of a comprehensive and objective definition of terrorism was the duty of Muslim scholars particularly. The definition reads as follows: "All acts of aggression committed by individuals, groups or states against human beings, including attacks against their religion, life, intellect and property, are terror acts" (Dorsey, 2001, p. 4). Apparently, this definition was not unanimously agreed upon, as after the conference one scholar commented that he felt that any act of violence or threat designed to terrorize people or endanger their lives or security constituted terrorism.

For Western diplomats, this description was far too broad and vague to be of much practical use. Many see the looseness of the definition as a way of allowing Muslim nations to brand Israel a terrorist state. In the U.S., not much was made of this process; in fact, one U.S. diplomat even commented that the efforts of the Muslim scholars would not have much of an impact on U.S. policy at all (Dorsey, 2001, p. 4).

While a rigorous definition fit for use in diplomatic circles has yet to be fully accepted, it is not hard to define terrorism from a visceral, emotional perspective. It is a power-hungry phenomenon that utilizes terror to kill, frighten, and intimidate. Terrorism makes people afraid to get up in the morning, apprehensive about their future, and distrustful of one another.

In a very real sense, it is a method of persuasion by force. It is a calculated mechanism, yet it feels no need of a logical rationale to justify its existence. Despite its madness, it cannot be ignored or left alone. William Pfaff (2002) of The Los Angeles Times wrote:

> Terrorism is a form of politico-military combat that attacks civilians for two reasons. First, the terrorists cannot get the political and military figures they really want to kill. Second, the terrorists kill civilians to frighten populations and force the leaders to compromise and make concessions to the terrorists' cause. (p. 8)

In other words, the terrorists believe that by killing civilians, they can obtain some concrete benefit.

And what of the victims? They are merely pawns, unlucky enough to be in the wrong place at the wrong time. The fact that they are absolutely innocent of anything that could possibly warrant their murder or mutilation deprives the victims of any free choice or emotional consent.

In this sense, terrorism possesses a strong will without any trace of ethics or morality; neither does it have a sense of guilt. Having no conscience, it does not have to justify anything to anyone. Rather, terrorists camouflage themselves, often with historical or religious motifs, in order to hide their faces. They show no remorse, self-esteem, or self-respect because they have merged their own individuality into that of the cause. They are always ready to fire the most potent weapon they have in order to intimidate and tyrannize society, namely their will to kill innocent people.

In the case of most radical Islamic terrorists, this merging of their own identity to a larger cause begins early on. As children they are schooled and indoctrinated to become militants of the Islamic liberation movements, the Jihad or Holy War, and "the rifle alone." Their mantra is "No negotiation, no conferences, and no dialogues." They want to achieve and restore Islamic glory not merely at any cost, but particularly through terror (Bergen, 2001, p. 7).

Islamic suicide terrorists work with three variables:
• The will to kill and be killed.
• The conviction of their reward in paradise.
• The conviction that they are acting as ambassadors of Allah.

These militants have no national flag or uniform; they cannot be easily identified. They go where they are asked to go and act as they are ordered. Their trademarks are the effect of surprise, sudden action, and secrecy. They have no control center from which they operate, yet they do know their sponsors. And they draw their strength from their religious convictions, praying at a mosque even if they have no other physical headquarters. They have no fear; what is there to worry about if Allah is on their side?

This is the common wisdom, but social analysts are starting to ask if it is really the case. The fact is, as one analyst put it, "We do not know how Muslim terrorists think" (Garton Ash, 2001, p. 21). We do know that they are educated and conditioned to die and kill helpless men, women, and children that they do not even know. While they wait to be called into action, they live praising the supposed martyrdom that prepares, motivates, and launches them to their own death by their killing of others. Nobel peace laureate Elie Weisel (2002) asserts that the only explanation for this behavior is "just plain hatred" (p. 15). He goes on to say, "Hate makes it strong and majestic. Terrorists harbour the will to impose their own law on large and small communities and to shame the helpless authorities" (p. 15).

Terrorism has become a human intercontinental missile that chooses its target according to its whim, from Beirut to Tanzania, from Kenya to Saudi Arabia. New York has only been the most symbolic target, but in the process of researching and writing this book, there have been several attacks carried out by Islamic fundamentalist groups. In April 2002, temples were bombed in Yerba, Tunesia, killing German tourists. In September, a French oil tanker was attacked off the coast of Yemen. On October 12, 180 people were killed in a terror attack in Bali. Finally, on October 26, Chechen terrorists took 700 people hostage in a Moscow theater. The rescue effort left over 100 people dead. What is next?

This is actually not such an unfathomable question, since there are several main radical Islamic terrorist groups whose preferred targets are well-known:

• Al Qaeda: Financed by Saudi millionaire Osama Bin Laden, this group's main target is the U.S.

• Yama al Islamiya: In existence since 1992, this group's main target is Egyptian industrial companies. Their biggest attack to date killed 158 foreign tourists along with four Egyptians near Luxor, Egypt in 1997.

• Jihad: This is another Egyptian terrorist group which has close ties to Al Qaeda. Its leader, Ayman Zawahri, was bin Laden's right-hand man. Jihad's main target is the U.S.

• The GIA (Islamic Armed Group): This group, based in Algeria, is responsible for the largest massacres in that country; over 100,000 people have been murdered at the GIA's hands. Al Qaeda has been known to use the group cells that the GIA has in Europe. This group's main target is the secular sector of Algeria, although they do not seem to be particularly picky about their victims.

• Hamas: Founded in 1987, this is the infamous suicide terrorist group in Israel. It has spawned the most dangerous terrorists in the world, promising its young suicide bombers a place in paradise, although the fact that their families generally receive substantial financial support may be another motivating factor. This group's main target is Israel.

• The Islamic Jihad: Another suicide terrorist group. It's main targets are Israel and the U.S.

• Hezbollah (The Party of God): This group, which operates out of Lebanon, has traditionally targeted U.S. facilities in Beirut and Israel. It receives financial support from both Syria and Iran, and has lately focused on Israel as its main target.

These are the best known terrorist groups, but others crop up, appearing and then merging or disappearing, all the time. The existence of such groups is well-documented, but what is unclear is what creates terrorists in the first place.

According to Marwan Bishara, a professor at the American University in Paris, terrorism is a manifestation of a vengeful inferiority complex. "When people feel so inferior militarily and economically, they adopt asymmetric means – not ordinary [ones] – to achieve what they want" (cited in Johnston, 2001, p. 6). The people who commit suicide attacks do so because they have nothing to lose and because they feel that it is the best way to cause as much damage to the enemy as possible. Bishara is quick to point out that poverty and misery alone do not create terrorists, although they may add to the problem: "It is a culture of defeat ... it is not just poverty, it is self-hatred; it is feeling inferior" (cited in Johnston, 2001, p. 6).

This definition fits perfectly with terrorist groups not only from the Third World, but also from the more industrialized countries as well. The IRA of Ireland and the Basque separatist group ETA in Spain are two examples of this theory that terrorism is an easy way to seek glory and make up for a feeling of inferiority. ETA's political and financial support organization, Batasuna, for example, has in the last several months been justified and practically glorified by the Bishops and over 200 priests in the Spanish Basque country. It is interesting to note that the Spanish Basque province, where nearly all of ETA's actions occur, is one of the wealthiest provinces in Spain, whereas the French Pays Basque, in which ETA is basically inactive, is one of the poorest in France. Poverty is clearly not a motivating factor here.

As for the IRA, its leaders came in front of television cameras on July 16, 2002, to apologize for the thousands of people they have felt compelled to kill in what have long been known as "The Troubles." This act, however, was public relations at its most cynical, nullified in short order when the IRA set off a bomb later that same month, causing yet another fatality in that endless conflict.

Terrorism is no laughing matter, yet the human condition is such that it needs to try to understand and analyze the incomprehensible. People who live in fear wonder where justice is, and how it is that so many terrorists act in the name of God and even receive support from recognized religious organizations. One joke making the rounds recently tells of a conversation between two men. The first asks if the priests, bishops, and Imams will consult with God to justify their support for terrorism. When the second man replies that he hopes not, the first asks him why not. The answer: God may agree with them. It is black humor, but taking into consideration the convictions of the terrorists who are ready to die for their cause, it rings eerily true.

six:

the war on terrorism

Life goes on without much change. There will be dramatic changes in the political climate that will involve our government more than others and it will require that we work together to put an end to the problem. I do not mean in a military sense but to find out what drives human beings to perform actions of that kind. We have to reflect before we act impulsively.
— Woody Allen (2001, p. 22)

THE WORLD WATCHED ATTENTIVELY TO see how the U.S. would conduct the war on terrorism in the wake of September Eleventh. One of the biggest shocks to come in the aftermath of the attacks was the realization of just how inefficient the supposedly state-of-the-art security agencies were. Put succinctly, Americans were dumbfounded by both the ignorance of the CIA and the passivity of the FBI.

The Central Intelligence Agency was born on the heels of

World War II in July, 1947. During the Cold War, it was considered to be extremely efficient and well-informed – feared throughout the world for its ability to gain access to state secrets and carry out covert actions. For the last ten years, however, analysts have accused the CIA of growing fat and losing its edge to become an agency full of bureaucrats who enjoy living in the affluent Virginia suburbs and working in carpeted, air-conditioned offices.

The CIA not only owes it to its own pride to pull itself up by the bootstraps, but more importantly, it owes it to the American people to rebuild itself and restore its credibility by doing a better job.

In this sense, an encouraging development took place after the September Eleventh attacks, when the CIA called for the need to work more closely with the FBI as well as the NSA (National Security Agency) and the NRO (National Recognizance Office). Dan Goure, from the Lexington Investigation Center put it bluntly, asserting that the fight against terrorism required an end to the "obnoxious rivalry among the Intelligence Agencies FBI, CIA, and NSA. Many times, they don't even share information with one another" (cited in: The U.S. information services... , 2001, p. 4). In fact, after the attacks, President Bush showed both surprise and not a little consternation at just how little the CIA and the FBI communicated with each other, expressing the opinion that only through cooperation and information sharing could he and his advisors get the best, most up-to-date information to make necessary decisions.

To add to the general dismay, most of the nation was appalled to find out just how little first hand information the CIA had garnered concerning Islamic terrorist groups. Several analysts, commenting on the agency's poor performance, ironically suggested that members of the CIA go to an army surplus store to buy some sturdy boots since they might actually have to start doing some heavy-duty leg work again. Looking at the number of shiny SUVs parked in the affluent suburbs of Washington, one can become downright cynical thinking how dirty those vehicles will get on the back roads they will need to travel to become acquainted with the terrorists' territories.

Joking aside, it is frightening to think of the lack of interest the agency has shown in sending agents to infiltrate the Taliban, Al Qaeda, or other Islamic terrorist groups. The move from the cocktail party atmosphere prevalent during the Cold War era to the desert cave era upon us now may prove too unappetizing to most CIA personnel. In fact, it has been alleged that there is probably not a single qualified agent of Middle Eastern background who speaks Arabic, never mind an agent who would be willing to spend years of his life playing the role of an Islamic fundamentalist, eating whatever he could get his hands on in the mountains of Afghanistan, the deserts of Africa or on an island in the Philippines, in order to glean information about a group like Al Qaeda.

This is, however, precisely what is needed in the war on terrorism. The salient information about such terrorist groups cannot be obtained from satellite images. It must be gained in the field, where agents would once again have to rely on information collected from human sources rather than relying solely on technology and computers. This is not a "smart war," but a messy one; as retired military officer and author Ralph Peters (2002) asserted, "The war against terrorism is a knife-fight to the bone" (p. A10).

President Bush seems to be aware that there will be no clean, speedy victory in this fight. But he also seems willing to go the distance: "We will be patient; this battle requires time and determination. Don't be mistaken; we will win. This will be a monumental combat of good against evil and good will prevail" (cited in: Gonzalez, 2001, p. 2). It was with this conviction that the president requested the support of America's allies to fight terrorism around the world.

In that moment right after the attacks, the clouds of unilateralism which had marked the first eight months of the Bush administration gradually dispersed. Article Five of the NATO (North Atlantic Treaty Organization) was invoked for the first time in 53 years, calling on members of the alliance to react to an attack against one of its members. And America's allies responded, echoing Bush's commitment and determination to fight terrorism, even as analysts predicted a catastrophic failure if the West invaded Afghanistan.

Despite the dire predictions, the U.S. military quickly demonstrated its intelligence, courage, and ability, as its troops progressively learned how to fight a well-trained enemy in difficult terrain and under extreme circumstances. Even with all its strategic and geographic advantages over the U.S. troops, the Afghan army, made up of Taliban and Al Qaeda fighters trained, in large part, with CIA methods, could not withstand the superior U.S. firepower. They were forced to abandon their political position and retreat to the remote mountainous areas of the country.

Unfortunately, the war on terrorism does not stop with this defeat. With the dismantling of the Taliban government, many of the Taliban who once ruled the country with an iron fist have receded back into normal civilian life. Al Qaeda, however, is still very much alive and operating in Yemen, Sudan, the Philippines, Georgia, as well as in several European countries, where the group seems to have found a sort of haven from which to plan its operations.

As was discussed in Chapter 4, Al Qaeda is organized into cells that are designed to dissolve and reform constantly. If a member is killed or apprehended, a new member from a dormant cell is added to the group so that its programmed operations may be continued seamlessly. With such a flexible and secretive organizational scheme, the infiltration, disarticulation, and destruction of the strategic group cells in order to destabilize Al Qaeda as a whole is a monumental task, one requiring not only military strength, but also intensive diplomacy, a well-honed intelligence service, and the support of all the allies the U.S. can muster to its cause.

With newfound determination driven by the will to seek some

sort of justice for the victims of September Eleventh, the U.S. will most certainly manage to smoke many Al Qaeda terrorists out of their usual lairs. And this is where the allies will be most important, for rather than going to their own countries for fear of being deported, many terrorists will choose to hide in Europe, counting on its reputation as a haven for terrorists.

The leaders of the European Union (E.U.) are aware that this is a major political problem for them; thus, they unveiled a battery of measures aimed at working with the U.S. to combat terrorism. The measures aim to detect and prevent financial transactions of suspected terrorists, as well as to investigate and suppress crime and terrorism in general. The measures were greeted lukewarmly by U.S. Secretary of State Colin Powell, who noted that they fell short of what the Europeans promised.

For one thing, the measures do not force local authorities to share information with their American counterparts. Powell noted, "It is hard to see how we can work together in criminal investigations without sharing personal data on suspects" (cited in: Taylor, 2001, p. 2). In addition, the European statesmen could not agree on a new form of arrest warrant to replace the cumbersome procedures which are currently in place to expedite an extradition. This slows the prosecution of terrorists down enormously.

Still, for all its limitations, the agreement is the first formal accord between the European Union and the U.S. to fight terrorism. It is to be hoped that the agreement will be improved and strengthened with time. Until then, many European countries have been working individually with U.S. officials to extradite those terrorists already held in connection with terrorist activities.

Apart from the judicial aspects of the war on terrorism, the financial front has been extremely active. The U.S. has made progress in squeezing the accounts of Al Qaeda and other terrorist groups; as one U.S. official noted, "They do not have the freedom they want. That is causing them some angst and difficulty" (cited in: O'Neil, 2001, p. 3). It is perhaps in this realm that the U.S. is receiving the most cooperation, with the financial institutions of many countries cutting their ties to terrorist groups and those that support them.

It is a daunting, almost impossible task to catch and prevent terrorist organizations from moving funds, many of which are coupled to legally established businesses, factories, and industries. This has been what police in countries like Spain, France, Germany, and England have found.

Still, for however lenient they may have been in the past, financial institutions throughout the world have taken seriously the warning of what consequences will befall them if they do not stop doing business with terrorist organizations. The United Arab Emirates, the Bahamas, the countries of the European Union, as well as most of the Asian countries have complied with the U.S. request to stop their dealings with terrorist fund raising institutions which have traditionally enjoyed protection under the protective umbrella of religious group status. Liechtenstein, a tiny European country whose financial institutions would not cooperate in the past, is now allowing U.S. investigators access to "trust funds" connected with the well-known Swiss organization TAQWA, known to help radical and fundamentalist groups. In another example of cooperation, Saudi Arabia, usually reluctant to go along with any plan related to terrorist organizations, has finally made public its willingness to comply with the U.S. request by implementing urgent laws against money laundering.

Along with eliminating the fund raising of these groups, however, the need to be able to detect and intercept financial transactions, which are the indispensable fuel for terrorist organizations, is paramount. Many Asian and Middle Eastern nations have developed independent intelligence units to deal with and fight financial crimes and to scrutinize charitable funds. The United Nations itself has recognized financial crime as an international phenomenon, adding that to stop this type of crime, the response must be international as well. As a result, the U.N. froze all the Al Qaeda accounts it could access.

Whereas the United Arab Emirates has moved quickly to do the same, Saudi Arabia has not been so eager to cooperate in this particular sphere. This should come as no great surprise since Saudi Arabia has been a traditional financial source for all violent Islamic movements. In any case, the pressure will continue to make the funding, either directly or indirectly, of such organizations a crime; indeed, although it will probably be accomplished out of the public eye, this stopping of the flow of money to terrorist groups is considered by most experts to be the necessary phase two of the war on terrorism (Sennott, 2002, p. 11). The movement in that direction is positive; nevertheless, on August 30, 2002, the U.N. reported that Al Qaeda still had enough money to operate as it sees fit.

Fighting terrorism is a task that is neither swift nor inexpensive. President Bush seems to understand this, defining the war on terror as a long term response to the world threat. The key is that this must indeed be a response, not merely a military task. As such, many political analysts are recommending the need to develop a multilateral effort to remedy the abysmal living conditions of countries whose misery and poverty are the perfect incubator for terrorists. When asked for examples, most analysts immediately point to the African nations.

Africa forms a sort of soft underbelly for global terrorists to take advantage of. For one thing, Islam is the fastest growing religion on the continent. In addition, vast numbers of Africans live in abject poverty. Africa is home to more than 100 million illiterate young people whose future is bleak, to say the least. They are hungry, dissatisfied with what convention has to offer them, on the edge of despair. This discontent is easily exploited by those who would recruit these young people for the Jihad or Holy War; although they are promised only hypothetical and other-worldly rewards, that is often sufficient inspiration to die for the terrorist cause.

Conversely, many analysts believe that if the poor nations of Africa were offered some real hope for the future, they would not be such a fertile breeding ground for terrorists. The International Institute for Strategic Studies in London, England, has criticized the lack of interest shown by the U.S. toward the needs of the world, especially for the poor and hungry. They feel that addressing these needs should be part of the general strategy in the war on terror. The Institute's latest report focuses on five main points:

1. The war on terrorism as carried out by the U.S. so far uses excessive military mobilization and too little economic and political commitment.

2. Bush's refusal to help rebuild countries after they have been swept of terrorists – Afghanistan, for example – is a serious strategic mistake.

3. The success against terrorism hinges on the ability to bring the fruits of democracy and capitalism to those who have never before had the privilege of enjoying them. The challenge is thus for politicians, not generals.

4. The U.S. is the only nation genuinely capable of giving a real forward push to the peace process in the Middle East. If the peace process were to succeed, it would help accomplish the U.S. objectives not only in the war against terrorism, but also in its quest to stop the proliferation of weapons of mass destruction. If the U.S. fails to help bring peace to the region, Arab regard for America will sink to nothing.

5. Finally, the U.S. must convince its allies, old and new, of the need to stay focused on a time-consuming and costly effort that seems suited to U.S. interests only. Again, this is a challenge for diplomats and politicians, not military personnel. Prados, 2002, p. 12).

Apart from advocating an effort on many fronts apart from the military one, the report predicts that there will most certainly be periodic tension between the U.S. and even its most stalwart allies in the prolonged effort to defeat terrorism. As new attacks are perpetrated, it becomes clear that "the war against terror requires Washington to build and lead a broad coalition using diplomatic as well as military tools and hold it together for many years to come" (The message in Bali, 2002, p. 6).

But why should such a coalition be so difficult to achieve? Shouldn't it be clear to everyone who the terrorists are and why they must be stopped? It is interesting to note that America's newfound determination to fight global terrorism contrasts sharply with the views of European intellectuals, political analysts, and social critics. In countries where nationalist groups have been involved in terrorist activities for decades, there is a certain feeling among intellectuals that so-called terrorists are merely a group of friends who got together with like-minded people to fight for an ideological cause which would have never gotten a fair hearing otherwise.

In England, a country proud of its democratic history, terrorism has been eulogized in Parliament for the last 30 years as political leaders talk endlessly of the courage of the martyrs in the Protestant or Catholic neighborhoods – the denomination depends on the speaker who currently has the floor. Meanwhile, the thousands of innocent victims who have been callously murdered in Northern Ireland are not generally regarded as martyrs.

Not to be outdone by their brothers in the homeland, many Irish Catholics in American cities like Boston join in the chorus of approbation by raising funds for the IRA. Since the IRA does not explode car bombs in their cities, those who raise the money cannot feel the pernicious effect their actions have.

Terror is also being canonized almost daily by many Basques in the Spanish Basque Country and the neighboring province of Navarre. In one instance, apologists for the cause of Basque independence actually used a city hall in that troubled province to have an official wake for three terrorists who were killed setting a car-bomb in a busy street. During the wake, the terrorists were praised as "martyrs of the cause." The Spanish government protested after this particular incident and in general tries to maintain a hard line against the Basque terrorist group ETA, but this group has long depended on the willingness of the French government to provide safe haven for its members as "political prisoners," even 25 years after the Franco regime gave way to a democratic government. Thus, many terrorists have been able to cross the border and enjoy a lovely meal while their innocent victims lie bleeding on the Spanish streets.

The Italians have the Red Brigade to answer for, the Greeks the November Seventeenth terrorist group, considered to be one of the most dangerous in Europe. The Germans have the dubious honor of having hosted the Bader-Meinhoff gang. And finally, there is the terrorism that has gone on within Israel since that nation was founded in 1947. As Palestinian terrorist groups try to achieve their goal of undermining the Israel's status, the Europeans, trying to appease the ever-larger pro-Palestinian groups in their own countries, ignore the problem and hope that it will just go away. After all, the English, French, and Germans created that particular mess in the first place; why should they feel compelled to find a just and lasting solution now?

The problem in understanding terrorism and terrorists is that it defies logic and ethics. In fact, terrorism is just a contemporary equivalent of Nihilism, a total lack of morality, wrapped in self-aggrandizing garments on which the names of innocent victims have been written in blood.

seven:
al quaeda and
the talibans

The U.S. is confronting an enemy in the shadows, a small,
effective, and anonymous terrorist army capable of cleverly
avoiding all detention systems.
— Javier Valenzuela (2001, p. 5)

AFTER THE AMERICAN BOMBING OF Afghanistan
which followed the September Eleventh attacks, Al Qaeda
was crippled in that country and disabled in Pakistan. Still, the
terrorist group has not been put out of business by any stretch of
the imagination. As one U.S. law enforcement official said, "They
are still capable of doing a lot of damage.... What we worry about
is that there are operations and its personnel are trained, organized,
and funded; they are simply waiting for the opportunity" (cited in:
Eggen & Dobbs, 2002, p. 1).

Al Qaeda, or "The Base" came into being in the 1980s as the
brain-child of Osama bin Laden. But bin Laden himself is a product of the misguided policies of the CIA and the Armed Forces

Spying Services during the war between Afghanistan and the former Soviet Union.

In 1979, the CIA made contact with bin Laden, who was twenty-two at the time and a student at the university of Jeddah. After his graduation in 1981, bin Laden reinitiated contact with the agency through the American embassy in Ankara, Turkey. At that point, he became a disciple of the CIA.

The agency trained him in the art of clandestine warfare and bin Laden proved to be a very good student. He learned how to prepare explosives, how to avoid detention, how to retreat to secure bases after a fast and fierce strike, how to move funds through false organizations and fiscal sanctuaries. Just how well he learned these lessons can be seen by the way he and his terrorist group Al Qaeda have been using these techniques to kill Americans and destroy American property around the globe. But that came later.

In the early 80s, before bin Laden's change of heart, he went to Peshawar, Pakistan, ostensibly as a representative of Saudi Arabia in Pakistan. In actuality he was working for the CIA. His mission: to help Afghan refugees fleeing the ravages of the war between their country and the USSR, and to raise funds for this purpose. He was successful at both, using his contacts in Saudi Arabia to do so. But bin Laden's mission started to change as he became involved in the recruiting of young boys – twelve to fourteen years old – refugees' children who were studying in the Madrasas, to become the child-soldiers of the Mujahidin.

Another assignment which bin Laden took very much to heart was the recruiting of Muslim volunteers from all over the Islamic world to help the Mujahidin fight against the Soviet army. Both assignments allowed bin Laden to forge solid contacts with Pakistani officials and Islamic fundamentalists from around the globe. These contacts in turn both inspired and aided him in forming his own "base" – Al Qaeda.

Apart from his personal fortune, which he inherited from his wealthy family, bin Laden was not above financing his organization with what could be considered "drug money." Indeed, a large part of the money that was pumped into Al Qaeda came from the cultivation of poppy seeds to produce morphine, the chemical basis for heroin.

The Islamic fundamentalist ideology of Al Qaeda was forged throughout the 1980s. One of the most important influences on bin Laden's way of thinking was undoubtedly his association with Abdullah Assam, a Palestinian who served as his ideological mentor at Jeddah University. Assam and bin Laden later fought together with the Mujahidin against the Soviets in Afghanistan and this association left an unmistakable impression on bin Laden. For its part, Al Qaeda, which served to recruit thousands of Islamic militants from many different Muslim states, gave a much needed boost to the Mujahidin, who went on to defeat the Soviet army. The routing of the USSR from an impoverished country such as Afghanistan was seen as an incredible victory for the entire Muslim world, and Al Qaeda's reputation was bolstered in turn.

The ideological underpinnings of bin Laden's brand of Islamic fundamentalism can be found in the rigorous Wahabi Doctrine. One of the characteristics of this doctrine is the refusal to accept any type of compromise with any political or social organization of a non-Muslim country, as these countries are considered the 'Infidel'. One of the most hated of the infidels, of course, is the U.S. In fact, the success of the Mujahidin, who were, in principle at least, backed by the U.S., actually worked against America. For behind the Mujahidin was Al Qaeda and its Islamic fundamentalist doctrine. Thus, hatred for the U.S. and its Muslim allies, who were seen by Al Qaeda as nothing more than unprincipled lackeys, heated up considerably.

In 1990, when the U.S. invaded Iraq after that country's attempt to overrun Kuwait, bin Laden's definitive change of heart against the U.S. was made known. He told the Saudi rulers in no uncertain terms that they had desecrated sacred Muslim land by allowing the American armed forces to be stationed at Saudi bases and use them to attack a fellow Muslim country.

Bin Laden's words were reported by political analyst Robert Fist: "We believe that God has used our "Holy War" the Jihad to destroy the Russian Army and now we ask God to use us again to defeat the United States of America and make it become its own shadow" (López Perona, 2001, p. 79).

Bin Laden believed that the liberation of Afghanistan was a holy duty for every Muslim. As the high priest of Al Qaeda, he urged its militants to continue the Jihad to liberate other countries.

In 1991, bin Laden was expelled from his native Saudi Arabia. Accused of antigovernment activities, he was stripped of his Saudi citizenship. He moved to Sudan, where he lived until 1996. While there, bin Laden and Al Qaeda were involved in the planning and execution of the terrorist attack against the World Trade Center on February 26th, 1993. The car bombing left six people dead and one thousand injured.

During bin Laden's five years in Sudan, Al Qaeda was also blamed for the suicide attack with a car bomb on a school building in Riyadh, Saudi Arabia, which killed six American teachers. In July 1996, the group was also responsible for the truck bomb at the U.S. military base in Dhahra, Saudi Arabia. In that attack, 19 American military personnel were killed and 400 were wounded.

In that same year, bin Laden was expelled from Sudan, which bowed to the intense pressure put on it by the U.S. government. It was then that bin Laden returned to Afghanistan, were he initially lived in a cave at the top of a mountain near Jahalabad. This was no ordinary cave, however. Rather, it was well-equipped with communications technology, allowing bin Laden to have contact to the outside world; indeed it was from this location in August 1996 that he launched the first declaration of the Jihad against the United States. The U.S. thus became an enemy to and a target for Islamic extremists.

Meanwhile, bin Laden was able to establish and finance Al Qaeda training camps in Afghanistan, Egypt, Sudan, Somalia, and Yemen. Finally, in 1997, bin Laden moved down from his mountain bunker to Kandahar, the headquarters of the Taliban leader Mohammed Omar. By the following year, he had found a niche for himself as an influential consultant to Omar and his Taliban government and as such, he became the strongest promoter of exporting the Taliban's fundamentalist ideology to neighboring countries. Obviously, Al Qaeda was to serve as the military arm of this proselytizing movement, carrying out the necessary military operations against the enemies of the Taliban.

The simultaneous bombings of the U.S. embassies in Kenya and Tanzania in the summer of 1998, which left 247 dead and hundreds more wounded, gave Al Qaeda an unprecedented prestige within the clerical circles of the Taliban. Steadily the armed forces of Al Qaeda became the knights of the Taliban government and the crusaders for Islamic fundamentalism around the globe.

In that same year, bin Laden met with his Al Qaeda captains in Kandahar. During this meeting, bin Laden issued an Islamic fatwa or decree, urging Muslims to kill Americans and their allies, civilians as well as military personnel. Calling the U.S. a "paper tiger," bin Laden was convinced that through concerted actions, American morale could be broken. The first such action was launched against the USS Cole, when a suicide boat bomb was rammed into the naval destroyer leaving 17 dead and 39 wounded.

Claude Lefort (2001), a French philosopher and political analyst has made some interesting comments about the crusaders of Al Qaeda. His insights are especially helpful to Westerners trying to understand the people behind this movement. First of all, Lefort asserts that the militants of Al Qaeda live with both a will to destroy and the willingness to suppress their own independent thinking. They are brainwashed to believe that they are emissaries of Allah with a mission to destroy evil and corruption. If they die performing their duty to faithfully fulfill this mission, they fully believe that as God's devout emissaries, they will have a place in paradise.

On an organizational level, Lefort emphasizes the fact that Al Qaeda consists of various group cells which operate in extreme secrecy. The members have no hierarchical ranks and their operations are decentralized to cause confusion and uncertainty to any outsider who tries to infiltrate the cell. This flexible organizational style gives Al Qaeda a tremendous advantage over a mammoth, bureaucratic organization such as the U.S. army. Concerning this advantage, former FBI counter-terrorist official Robert Blitzer commented, "This network is so organized and broad, it won't take them that long to get retooled" (cited in Eggen & Dobbs, 2002, p. 14).

Their religious fervor gives Al Qaeda members the motivation to go beyond any foreseeable limitations. The group has the ability to carry out terrorist attacks anywhere in the world. As journalist Thomas Fuller (2002) pointed out, "There are people connected with Al Qaeda who have been trained and are awaiting their call to action" (p. 4).

Keeping all this in mind, it would be a mistake to believe that the capture or doing away with bin Laden would lead to the disappearance of Al Qaeda and its group cells. Unfortunately, the ingredients to produce another bin Laden-style leader are found in abundance in the Middle East. For example, while the fate of bin Laden himself remains a mystery, another Al Qaeda member, Abu Zabaydah, has emerged as a new leader. Fortunately, this elusive thirty-year-old Palestinian has already been caught and arrested. But another report dating from July of 2002 indicated that bin Laden's son has already taken the reins of Al Qaeda.

And all the while, Al Qaeda seems to be continuing its perpetration of terrorist acts. While none have been as spectacular as the events of September Eleventh 2001, they have still caused fatalities. In April, 2002, seventeen tourists, eleven of them Germans, died as a result of a terrorist attack on a synagogue in Yerba, Tunesia.

Indeed, several other synagogues and Jewish cemeteries have been subject to terrorist attacks and it may not all be attributable to one group. Still, the German defense minister acknowledged a link between the attack in Yerba and Al Qaeda's group cells. Most recently, on May 13, 2003, the Riyadh compounds in Saudi Arabia were attacked by suicide terrorists; eight Americans were among the thirty-four people killed there. Another attack attributed to Al Qaeda's group cells was that launched on May 17, 2003, when 14 suicide terrorists led five different attacks in Casablanca, Morocco, leaving forty-three people dead.

The numerous attacks since September Eleventh, from Bali to Casablanca, lead to the obvious conclusion that even with bin Laden dead or in hiding, Al Qaeda is still very much alive and able to attack. George Tenet, director of the CIA, is of the opinion that not only does the terrorist group have the motivation, but also that they still have to means to hurt U.S. interests again (Gaztelu, 2002, p. 4).

THE TALIBAN

AFGHANISTAN, A COUNTRY COMPRISING many different tribal societies and political factions, has a long history of civil war. The Soviet invasion of the country in 1979 briefly galvanized the Afghanis, who joined together against the foreign enemy. However, when the Soviet troops withdrew from Afghanistan, leaving the country desolate and humiliated after ten years of warfare, the various factions once again turned toward fighting amongst themselves.

This situation did not go unnoticed by the Pakistani secret service, ISI. They formulated one clear objective concerning their neighbor and went about accomplishing that objective in a most intelligent way: through education.

At the time, many Afghan refugees were present in Pakistan.

The host country took in the children of these mostly Pashtun refugees and educated them in the Madrasas, or Koranic schools in Pakistan.

These schools flourished from 1979, supported by both the U.S. government and Saudi Arabia. Many of these boarding schools were established specifically for the children of Afghan refugees who had fled from the horrors of war in their home country.

A good number of these children had previously served as soldiers in the era of the Mujahidin. Now they would be used by the Pakistanis to support a government back in their homeland, a government which would best serve the interests of Pakistan. They became the "hard core" students, or Taliban, inculcated in the fundamentalist Wahabi doctrine within the Deobandi movement.

The Wahabi interpretation of Islam, as expounded by Muhammad Abd-ul Wahab in the 18th Century, calls for the purification of the Islamic faith. The founder preached the need to "suffocate and rot out the infidel who would seek to create equal partners to Allah" (Elorza & Elorza, 2001, p. 21). For its part, the Deobandi movement seeks to purify Islam by purging it of past influences and returning it to the basic texts of the Koran and the Hadiths (Proverbs) of Mohammed the Prophet.

The Madrasa schools were the perfect breeding ground for soldiers for the new Jihad. The students professed blind obedience to their teachers, or Mullahs. They were trained to respond to their teachers' call to the Jihad as the will of God. In this they were supported by their families, although many are fully aware that the call to Jihad may end in death. One father of a student at a Madrasa, when asked if he wasn't afraid that his son might fall as a warrior against the Northern Alliance, responded, "I support the Jihad. I would love to have a Shaheed [martyr] son" (cited in: Goldberg, 2001, p. 7).

The malleability of the Taliban students obviously had much to do with the continued turmoil and infighting rampant back in their own country. They were looking for a leader to inspire them, and in the end they found one in a rural clergyman and former warrior who had fought against a band of Mujahidin who had been terrorizing the countryside. The clergyman managed to bring about law and order over the group and restore a measure of tranquility to the region. The hardcore Taliban had found someone to follow. The man in question was Mohammed Omar. Born in 1959, he had fought against the Soviet Union and its satellite government in Kabul. In 1996, riding on the wave of support afforded him by the Taliban, he became the leader of Afghanistan. He and the Taliban seized power representing a movement of order and renewal against the anarchy and corruption caused by the presence of more than 180 tribal leaders. He later took Osama bin Laden into his circle of advisors and offered both bin Laden and his terrorist group Al Qaeda a secure refuge and base of operations.

The problem for Omar, and in turn, for bin Laden, was that the absence of a political formation within the Taliban movement – along with the extreme formulation of their socio-religious doctrine – failed to integrate the Afghani people into the new system. In a sense, then, the Taliban's progressive radicalization of the country forced its leaders to put Afghanistan's destiny into the hands of international terrorists like bin Laden. Thus, the Taliban government, initially accepted by many, lost its international support by creating a universally hostile and intolerable environment.

The Taliban regime is gone now, forced to flee by the American bombings. However, they are still a violent force, with many Taliban in the mountainous regions of Afghanistan, waiting for another opportunity. Needless to say, America is still their most hated enemy; they consider the U.S. to be imperialist bearers of corruption throughout the world. The Jihad against such corruption is thus still regarded by the Taliban as the absolute duty of every Muslim.

As for their legacy, the Taliban will most probably be remembered more for their repressive actions than for the discrete points of their theology. The brutal destruction of the ancient Buddhist statues in Bamiyan will be difficult to forget as will the heartless repression of women under their medieval style regime.

It is, however, important to bear in mind that even though they are no longer in power, the philosophy that drove the Taliban is still the center of attention in many Islamic countries. In fact, the Deobandi movement can claim for itself the most popular type of religious education in the Muslim world, with numerous schools in every Islamic country. The West has not heard the last of Islamic fundamentalism.

eight:
islam

We need to resist the idea that the Islamic world is somehow culturally incapable of development. There is a tremendous opportunity to bring globalization to places that have not seen much of it.
— Development expert Jeffrey Sachs (cited in: Kahn, 2002, p. 13)

TINGED WITH SHADES OF EXOTICISM and fear, Islam is a vast unknown quantity to most Westerners. It is, however, quickly becoming familiar to Americans and Europeans alike as immigration brings increasingly larger numbers of Muslims to the affluence of North America and Europe. Just what does this religion, the fastest growing faith in the world, entail?

In essence, Islam, which means "submission" in Arabic, is a fairly simple faith supported by several fundamental doctrines. The first is a strict monotheistic doctrine, similar to that of Judaism or Protestantism, which forbids the worship of any object or being other than Allah, or God. This is fundamental to every one of the numerous sects and fragmentations of the Muslim faith. The other main figure of the faith is Mohammed, the prophet, who is seen as Allah's messenger.

The practice of Islam centers on the Arkan al-Islam, the prayer that is said facing the holy city of Mecca five times a day. It is a recitation of the five pillars of the faith, which are the five duties every believer must carry out in order to go to "the Garden" or paradise. These duties are as follows:

1. The Sha Hada or profession of faith.

2. The Salat, or prayer which is recited facing the holy city of Mecca five times a day.

3. The Sakah, or giving of alms.

4. Saum, or fasting during the month of Ramadan, with is the ninth month of the lunar calendar.

5. The pilgrimage to the holy city of Mecca at least once in a believer's lifetime.

To this list of five duties, some radical Islamic theologians have added that of the Jihad, or holy war. Needless to say, the inclusion of the Jihad is not accepted by every Muslim scholar or believer.

The holy book of the Muslim faith is the Koran, which Muslims believe to have been revealed exclusively and in its entirety by Allah, who delivered this message to the angel Gabriel. It is thus believed that the original copy of this sacred book is kept in heaven. Even so, its earthly counterparts are considered holy objects and the desecration of any copy of the Koran is a crime punishable by death.

Of course, the Koran is a text with a long history. Its compilation as a unified text occurred during what is known as the Third Caliphate in the years 644 to 656 A.D.. It assumed its current form as a written manual or scriptio in the years between 694 and 714 under the leadership of the Islamic scholar Hadiadi-Ibn-Yusef of Iraq. While it remains the authoritative holy book of the Islamic faith, it is complemented by the Jadiz, a rich collection of quotations from Mohammed the Prophet.

The Koran itself basically describes the spiritual, social, and political evolution of Mohammed the Prophet from the years 610 to 630, the year of his death. The most salient date of this evolution is July 15, 622, which marked the turning point both in the Prophet's personal life and in the history of Islam. On that date, Mohammed the Prophet left Mecca and traveled to Medina (in what is now Saudi Arabia) and was thus transformed from a purely religious figure to a political one, a statesman of sorts. This transformation produced a subsequent change in both the tone and content of the Prophet's revelations, which became increasingly related to social and political issues. Some of the new revelations even conflicted with the Prophet's previous ones, but it was the new revelations which became law. For example, polygamy was legalized and the position of women was devalued in comparison to that of men.

Apart from changing the rules governing social structures, these new revelations also altered the political balances of the era. In his dream to control more territory and expand the dominion of the faith, Mohammed the Prophet justified the use of violence. The acceptance of hostility toward the infidel thus began. Moreover, the Prophet promised celestial rewards to those who died in battle against the enemy.

After his death in 632, Mohammed was succeeded by his son-in-law, Umar, known as the First Caliph. During his rule from 634 to 644, Umar expanded the domain of Islam beyond the Arabian Peninsula to Egypt, Syria, Iraq, and Mesopotamia. What could be called the dynasty of Mohammed the Prophet, during which all the caliphs were directly related to the Prophet himself, lasted until 661.

During the next hundred years, from 661 to 750, Islam had one of the most radiant periods in its history. This era began with Muawiya, the governor of Syria, who started the Omeya dynasty. During this period, the Muslim faith and culture expanded its dominion, stretching from Spain to Central Europe and even all the way to China. Despite all its new-won territory, however, the real power remained in the hands of families of Arabic origin who had some form of relation to Mohammed the Prophet. This was the case up until the 10th Century.

Whereas the Omeya dynasty produced a golden age of Muslim culture, the Ottoman Empire (1325-1600) provided Islam with its most politically successful period. During this time, the Ottoman Turks were the most feared power in the world, a veritable nightmare banging on the gates of Vienna, ready to overrun European Christendom. The Empire's progress was only slowed (and eventually stopped) by the Spanish Armada with support from Spain's naval allies from Venice and the Vatican.

The decline of Islam's influence began in the late 1500s with the collapse of the Ottoman Empire. The Muslims were expelled from Spain, Central Europe, and other territories, in which new, non-Muslim leaders were quick to seize power, sometimes to destroy, other times to take over the legacy the Muslims left behind.

This legacy is rich indeed, including as it does scientific, architectural, and agricultural developments, as well as an uncanny ability to adapt and perfect foreign innovations. In Spain, for example, the Muslims brought their knowledge of logic, mathematics, and engineering to bear fruit, cultivating art and poetry along with new crops like rice and oranges and basically saving Spain from the plunge into what the rest of Europe experienced as the Dark Ages. It should be noted, however, that while modern historians have many practical explanations for the great progress of Islam in its early history, Muslims themselves have always attributed the success of their culture to a supernatural force.

Be that as it may, the spread of Muslim culture only came upon the heels of military conquests, which in turn spawned the process of conversion to the Islamic faith. Early on within the conquered territories other religions were tolerated, albeit begrudgingly. Those who did not convert were obliged to pay dues to the new rulers.

And always, sooner or later, the choice was between conversion or death.

To this day, Islam is not a religion which cohabitates well with other faiths. Followers of Islam are prohibited from abandoning their faith and most Muslim states forbid the proliferation of other religions within their boundaries. In addition, Muslim states are just that; there is no separation between church and state and Koranic law is binding.

These conditions make Islam a religion that commands obedience and leaves little room for debate and individual decision making. This philosophy has also made it difficult for non-Muslims to live in Muslim countries. It was perhaps this intolerance that caused the anti-Muslim backlash in the countries that had been occupied during the golden age of Islam. Whatever the cause, the fact is that after one thousand years of military triumph and political power, by the early 1600s, Islam was forced to retreat to its original dominions under a cloud of defeat and humiliation. The ultimate humiliation came two hundred years later, though, when the Muslim nations became colonies of the French and British empires.

For most of the 20th Century, the Islamic countries wrapped themselves even further in religion, in part to conceal their problems and in part to console themselves for these problems. Many countries claim to be the exclusive representatives of Allah's unquestionable and infallible word, even though this claim has put them at odds with one another. Still, one commonality among the Islamic regimes, which tend to be heavily influenced by their priests or Ulamas, is a general animosity toward the West. There are, perhaps, some genuine reasons for the Islamic world to bear a grudge against the more industrialized nations, but oftentimes it is merely a diversionary tactic to take people's minds off their real problems. Thus, the U.S. and Europe have become the major culprits for the unhealthy economy in the Arab world, as well as for the general lack of development, the staggering illiteracy rate, the crushing poverty, the undemocratic political systems, and the absence of human rights so prevalent in Muslim countries. The Ulamas, by putting the blame squarely on the shoulders of others, thus avoid having to make real changes to solve the problem.

As is the case in other religions, Muslim priests are basically self-appointed. They have always had a powerful influence on laypeople as well as on those in positions of worldly authority, but in previous eras, the Ulama was a multifaceted figure. Not only was he supposed to be a learned theologian, but he was also expected to be an expert in other disciplines as well. Nowadays, the Ulamas have become overtly, and perhaps overly, political. They shun all knowledge and education which extends beyond the fundamental principals of Islam; unfortunately, they are not particularly well-versed in the complex nuances of their own religion either. This has made them defensive and overly authoritarian; many are afraid that their simplistic, often controversial views and interpretations of Islam might be questioned by educated laymen and this, of course, would greatly undermine an Ulama's authority. The fact that Islam has no papal-type figure nor hierarchy similar to that of the Catholic church, for instance, exacerbates this problem, as an Ulama need not answer to any higher authority.

This is not to say that Islam is an anti-intellectual faith. Indeed, throughout its history, Islam has produced great scholars in all branches of learning and science. The current political and religious climate, however, does not bode well; most historians and analysts are in agreement that the future of the Islamic world looks dim, with no glimmer of great improvements in its economy, educational systems, or human rights records in sight.

Like many other religions, Islam is more than a matter of faith. Rather, it is a comprehensive way of life. Within the boundaries it delimits, it has the means and teachings to enhance the spiritual values of its believers and to bring stability and prosperity to the Muslim countries. The doctrine contained in the Koran can be an incredibly positive, creative force to motivate Muslims to work toward improving their situation. Unfortunately, the call of many "deviant" Ulamas to depend solely on divine help will not help achieve any progress in developing new infrastructures, clearing the way for democratic reforms, or progressing on the issue of human rights. The isolationism of the last fifty years has left the Muslim world out of the globalization loop. Muslim countries have missed opportunities to open their horizons and borders. They have failed to attract foreign investment. Indeed, they are mired down in their own system.

For the leaders of most Muslim countries, this is not a problem to be solved. Most Islamic countries are governed by non-democratic regimes that fear the political upheaval that could come on the heels of development and progress. This explains the reluctance of most Muslim leaders to instigate or even think about any kind of social changes. They are afraid of spoiling the religious and political status quo that camouflages their own corrupt system.

That being said, some more liberal Muslim leaders have begun to recognize the need to change the educational system by introducing more secular education and especially technological education. But a whole slew of changes is needed to bring any kind of lasting stability to the area. Muslim countries need to change their legal structures to guarantee foreign investment and the influx of capital they so desperately need. To do this, they must move toward more democratic systems of government, not the kind of charade of an election in which 100% of the population eligible to vote unanimously elects a dictator like Sadam Hussein.

Of course, some attempts have been made to stimulate development, but such efforts only make some radical, fundamentalist organization emerge, urging the return to the original Islamic doctrine as written in the Koran. They cloak their demands, which are little more than a will to maintain their own power, with talk of how Western ways will corrupt Islamic culture and civilization.

If it were only talk, the problem would be minimal. Unfortunately, radical fundamentalist movements have always leaned heavily on violence and terror to get their point across. A glance at Muslim history gives evidence of the existence of violent sects as early as the 12th Century. But such movements burgeoned under colonialism so that by the 1900s, numerous ideological movements calling for the establishment of an Islamic state had surfaced. They felt that this was the only way to halt the decadence of Muslim civilization.

One of the most well-known movements was that of the "Muslim Brothers," founded in Egypt in 1928 by Hasan al-Banna (1906-1949). Al-Banna was one of the first advocates for the implantation of an Islamic state. The Muslim Brothers, however, became even too adamant for Al-Banna, who was killed by some of his more radical followers in 1949.

Another renowned ideologist of the beginning of the 20th Century was Addel Kader Awda, who prompted a return to the Sharia, or Koranic law. The fact that modern Arab nations had been moving away from the strict observation of the Sharia can be seen by the fact that Awda was condemned to death and executed under the orders of Egyptian leader Abdel Nasser in 1954.

Meanwhile, farther east in Pakistan, there were increasing calls to establish an Islamic state in that part of the world. One of the main advocates for this cause was Abdul Ala Mawdudi (1903-1980). Mawdudi promoted the formation of an Islamic state under the concept of Hakimiya, or divine sovereignty. This was a direct response to the ignorance of the West in matters of the Islamic faith, as well as the secularization promoted by Western civilization.

Mawdudi, who was the main ideologist behind the concept of an Islamic Revolution, made a major contribution to the doctrine behind the practical conclusions reached during the struggle of the Muslims to break away from India in 1947. For his part, Mawdudi was influenced by the Egyptian Said Qotb (1906-1966), who is credited with having developed the modern-day radical Islamic ideology.

Qotb, as it turns out, was a well-known member of the Muslim Brothers. Accused of intending to assassinate President Nasser of Eygpt in 1956, Qotb, like Awda, was condemned to death. Throughout his life, however, Qotb had defended the Sharia as an expression of the divine will of Allah.

Radical Muslim ideology in general, and Qotb in particular, had a large part in spawning the terrorist attacks perpetrated by radical followers of Islam in the Arab world as well as in the U.S. and other Western countries. As the founder of Islamic Jihad, Qotb can basically be considered the father of most present-day Islamic terrorist organizations.

There are, however, more players on the stage. One is Mustafa Chukri, the founder of the terrorist organization known as "The Immigration." He defends violence as the only means to defeat the corrupted states that do not truly believe.

Addeslam Faraj, the cofounder of the Islamic Jihad, is another important figure in the radical movements. He introduced and advocated what he called the "supreme form" of combating evil, namely suicide terrorism. He did this by convincing his followers that their calling and duty was to die to make Islam reign. For Faraj, the fight against tyrannical states and infidel societies is part of the divine will of Allah.

The continuous terrorist attacks carried out by Islamic radicals began in 1979 with the attack on Mecca, Saudi Arabia, in which thousands of Muslim pilgrims died. In 1980, the Muslim Brothers of Egypt inaugurated the Jihad, as well as the first Intifada in Palestine to fight both for a Palestinian state and against Israel. Since that time, the radical fundamentalist ideology has spawned numerous violent groups: Hamas in Palestine, Hezbollah (The Party of God) in Lebanon, the MIA (Islamic Armed Movement) and GIA (Islamic Armed Group) in Algeria, the PLO (Palestine Liberation Organization), and many more.

One hallmark of these groups has been that, despite their constant pressure, they have not achieved their goals. Still, this did not stop the creation of Al Qaeda, which was initially founded to recruit soldiers from the entire Muslim world to fight in Afghanistan. In fact, Al Qaeda was originally supported by both Saudi Arabia and the U.S. as a way of defeating the Soviet army. Once it became obvious, however, that the Soviets would withdraw from Afghanistan, it did not take long for the members of Al Qaeda to turn their weapons upon those who had helped them get started in the first place, especially the U.S. The Gulf War, which came as a response to Sadam Hussein's invasion of Kuwait, only sharpened the hatred for America felt by Al Qaeda members. Now, along with the U.S., most of the West is considered a target of aggression. It was in this atmosphere that Osama bin Laden, currently the most infamous terrorist in the world, consolidated his power, supported by his own personal fortune as well as by Saudi Arabian fundamentalists.

The Islamic world, however, is not a monolith any more than the Western world is. Numerous advocates of democratic values have come to the fore in many Muslim countries in the past decades, famous ideologists who call for the incorporation of democratic alternatives into Islamic doctrine. They include Rachid Ganuchi of Tunesia, Addelilah Benkiran of Morocco, and Majfud Nannah of Algeria, to name a few. Still, these individuals seem like voices crying in the wilderness, overshadowed by the autocratic governments in their countries which refuse to initiate changes toward democratic systems, promote human rights, and open the doors for progress.

Analyst Thomas Friedman (2002) noted the paradoxical situation in Saudi Arabia, where 55% of the young people want to leave their oil-rich country to seek better opportunities elsewhere. This statistic is underscored by the boats that land almost daily on the Mediterranean beaches of Europe, bringing desperate immigrants from Northern Africa to Spain and Italy. The fact that these people risk their lives seeking a better life in a totally unknown and foreign country illustrates the anguish, frustration, and tragedy of the present-day Muslim world. As one middle class Saudi asserted, "The problem here is not Islam. The problem is too many young men with no job and no university and nowhere to go except to the mosque" (cited in: Friedman, 2002, p. 9). Once there, radical preachers fill their heads with anger for America.

There are 1.300 million Muslims in the world today; in fact, one out of every five people on the planet follows the Islamic faith. It is the fastest growing religion in the world, mostly in poor countries that cannot support this kind of population growth. The majority of Muslims are as peace-loving as any average Westerner. Yet the handful of radical fundamentalists are enough to cause very grave problems, not only for their own countrymen, but for the rest of the world.

These problems stem in large part from the fundamental differences in the values of Islamic radicals with those of the Western world. Some of these differences are as follows:

• Radical Muslims do not believe in democracy. Westerners do.

• Radical Muslims do not believe in freedom of religion. Westerners do.

• Westerners believe that Muslims have the right to proselytize in western nations. Radical Muslims persecute and kill those who promote other religions in their countries.

• Radical Muslims demand monolithic uniformity. Westerners believe in pluralism.

• Radical Muslims believe that the laws were delivered by Allah and that they are therefore unchangeable. Westerners believe that the laws are created by men; therefore they can be changed.

• Westerners believe in freedom of the press. Radical Muslims do not.

• Westerners believe that men and women should have equal rights under the law. Radical Muslims do not.

• Westerners believe in free education for both men and women.

Radical Muslims do not.

• Westerners do not believe that minors should be militant soldiers. Islamic fundamentalists do.

• Westerners help Muslims when they are victims of oppression or in need. Radical Muslims are not willing to help the infidel, even when they are victims of extreme poverty or misery.

It is in the interest of all moderate Muslims as well as the West to make sure that Islamic fundamentalists do not take complete control of the Muslim world, for if they do, there will never be peace between that world and ours.

nine:
the nuclear threat

RECENTLY, THE CIA CREATED a prognosis for the state of the world in the year 2015. This hypothetical "report card" raises an alarm about the proliferation of weapons of mass destruction among terrorist organizations and groups of organized crime. Unfortunately, while this may sound alarmist, it is not all that far-fetched.

On several occasions in the late 1990s, media reports warned that the black market for radioactive materials had doubled in the last half of that decade. The lack of control over such a market means that not only is it possible that radioactive materials could fall into the hands of suicide terrorist eagerly seeking such weapons, but that it is entirely plausible.

In the last decade of the 20th Century, the membership of the "Nuclear Club," those countries that have nuclear weapons in their military arsenals, had increased to include both India and Pakistan. These are two of the developing nations actually known to have atomic weapons; there are probably several others who have managed to keep their weapons programs secret.

What is the problem with these nations having weapons of mass destruction? One look at what the Pakistani Minister of Science, Mr. Attaur Rahman, said in his proclamation speech during the celebration of the first nuclear explosion test on May 28, 1998, provides an unsettling answer: "We bow our heads before Allah, the Almighty, because the greatness of Pakistan has been restored" (cited in: Goldberg, 2001, p. 7). These words may be a mere formality, but they have an eerie ring of sincerity.

The fact is that Pakistani militants have become increasingly radical, thanks in large part to the popular school system of the Madrasas (see Chapter 7 for more details about these schools). Moreover, these radicals, whose thinking is rooted in fundamentalist Islamic beliefs, contend that Pakistan's nuclear weapons ought to form a part of the arsenal of the Jihad (Goldberg, 2001, p. 7).

This rhetoric naturally disturbs most of the non-Islamic world, especially since the weapons could very well fall into the hands of fundamentalists and radical Muslims during some kind of violent revolt, which is not an uncommon occurrence in Pakistan. When asked whether the world should worry about Pakistan's nuclear arsenal, Pervez Musharraf, Pakistan's political and military leader, responded that it was totally impossible that the weapons fall into the hands of irresponsible people. He further added,

> We believe that God is the supreme king and we are his representatives on earth; everything has to be done according to the teaching of Allah. When we say "the will of God," it does not mean we cannot or will not use our brains. People should not imagine that because we are fundamentalists, we are going to blast a nuclear bomb at the first opportunity.
> [Cited in: Musharraf descuenta…, 2002, p. 12)

As soothing as these words are meant to be, they do little to diminish the anxiety of the Western countries uncomfortable with the idea that Allah is the founder of Pakistan's nuclear program.

This concern has grown considerably as the conflict between Pakistan and India over the region of Kashmir heats up. In an interview with the German news magazine *Der Spiegel*, Musharraf did not exclude the use of nuclear weapons in his country's conflict with India, saying:

> The blood flows through our hearts. The Pakistani people are fully sympathetic with the resistance of the popular movements in Kashmir. We act with responsibility and I am optimistic that we can defend ourselves with conventional weapons. Only under the threat of Pakistani extinction will the pressure of our people force the government to make use of our atomic weapons. (Cited in: Pervez Musharraf..., 2002, p. 6)

Later during the interview, Musharraf confirmed that Osama bin Laden had made contact with one of Pakistan's nuclear scientists and that the leader of Al Qaeda never got close to his dream of possessing his own nuclear weapons – a small consolation in a world where change occurs so rapidly.

Addressing the issue of the proliferation of nuclear arms in his first State of the Union address, George W. Bush made mention of the "Axis of Evil Nations" – Iraq, Iran, and North Korea – as countries capable of producing weapons of mass destruction as well as the missiles to launch them. North Korea is, according to a CIA report, known to have one, possibly two, nuclear warheads and transcontinental missiles capable of reaching Hawaii or Alaska. That same report contends that North Korea also has chemical and biological weapons programs along with the ability to produce ballistic missiles. Even more frightening is the fact that the impoverished nation is eager to earn some money selling the technology.

According to the same CIA report, Iran does not currently possess nuclear weapons, although they have chemical and biological weapons programs and the capability to build intercontinental missiles.

In the case of Iraq, Saddam Hussein's plan to build a nuclear facility for military purposes was stymied when the installations, which had reached an advanced stage, were bombed by the Israelis in 1981. A decade later, U.S. and British air force planes destroyed the remaining facilities. Of course, Iraq's ability to produce chemical and biological weapons along with the missiles to launch them is well-documented. Iraq, however, was under constant surveillance by the U.S. and Great Britain since its government repeatedly refused to abide by the U.N. resolutions made after the failed attempt to annex Kuwait. The most glaring example was Iraq's refusal to allow U.N. weapons inspectors into the country; after intense pressure, that stance changed, but it was not enough to avoid armed conflict with the U.S.

An enormous problem that receives little attention from the news media concerns the arsenal of the former Soviet Union. Greenpeace representatives have visited several Russian nuclear installations, all of which failed miserably in the area of protection against terrorism. Nuclear residue is accessible to the public with little difficulty; in fact, a terrorist could trigger an explosion one thousand times larger than the meltdown at Chernobyl. Unfortunately, the former USSR has neither adequate security measures nor sufficient financial means to buy back or import used nuclear waste from the nations formed after the disintegration of the Soviet Union. Even a Russian deputy, Sergei Mitrojin, had to admit that Russia has yet to learn how to manipulate nuclear waste.

Still, Russian experts maintain that their nuclear arsenals are safe from terrorists. Alexei Yablokov, director of the Russian Ecological Center, confirmed that now, ten years after the break-up of the Soviet Union, the nuclear arsenal in the area is under strict control. In contrast, a recent independent report stated that at least 60% of Russian nuclear material was not properly safeguarded. Several times, radioactive material of Russian origin has landed on the black market. As recently as June 2000, four pounds of enriched uranium turned up in Butumi, Georgia, on the Black Sea. This discovery triggered new fears of more nuclear material being traded on the black market. Russian officials are quick to deny any lack of security. In fact, this incident, along with a previous one in 1994, prompted Vladimir Tomarouski, speaking for the Russian Federal Security Service, to accuse the international press of publishing these occurrences merely to spread negative propaganda against Russia (Goldberg, 2001).

Although experts say that this type of radioactive material has no military application, it does not cease to be unnerving that such material is not under the strictest of controls. Thus, the U.S. has joined forces with its former arch-enemy to create programs to reinforce the security of Russian nuclear installations as well as to stop the "brain drain" of experts and scientists from the country itself. Both countries have forged an international consensus on the need to prevent Russia's weapons of mass destruction from falling into the hands of terrorists or mafia organizations. Even President Bush, who seemed ready to pull funding for the programs, has decided to continue them as a way to prevent terrorism.

JUST HOW REAL IS THE THREAT OF NUCLEAR TERRORISM?

ALEXEI YABLOKOV, DIRECTOR OF THE Radioactive and Nuclear Security Program feels that the threat can only be realized if a nuclear center is attacked directly. As for the making of a nuclear bomb, Yablokov feels that it is impossible without expert scientists, laboratories, and a lot of time, although any country that already has nuclear power plants can use the knowledge needed to run such installations to make an A-bomb. The production of a sophisticated nuclear bomb, however, requires special technology and expertise that only few countries have. Precisely for this reason, the Russians are very concerned about the so-called "brain drain," or flight of scientists and technology from their country.

After reviewing the facts, the Greenpeace energy department, headed by Maxin Shingarkin, concluded that there are no nuclear weapons out of control in the former Soviet Union, nor any foundation to the supposition that a terrorist group has been able to obtain the raw materials needed to make an atomic weapon. Still, there is cause for great concern. For one thing, Russian military leader Aleksandr Lebed has spoken several times about the disappearance of several dozens of "suitcase" nuclear bombs. The General even mentioned the size of the cases: 60 x 40 x 20 centimeters.

This information was first released to the American public in October 2001, even though the U.S. government had been aware of it since September Eleventh, 2001. Apparently, the media had been asked to delay publication to avoid confusion and even more panic. Later, after it was published, the information was discounted as lacking in factual evidence, especially since the Russian Minister of Atomic Energy denied that such suitcase bombs had ever existed.

Whatever happened, the fact remains that there are thousands of nuclear warheads, thousands of pounds of highly enriched uranium, and hundreds of tons of highly enriched plutonium (used for military purposes) in the hands of the weak governments that were created after the disintegration of the Soviet Union. This, along with the presence of the enormous arsenals of chemical and biological weapons within the territory of the former USSR should give us all pause.

DOES THE WORLD HAVE TO WORRY ABOUT THE "DIRTY BOMB"?

TERRORIST ORGANIZATIONS THAT USE suicide terrorists to meet their objectives will definitely be willing to use "dirty" bombs even if the nuclear material may not be rich enough to kill a single human being. While not being directly lethal, such a bomb would cause dangerous levels of contamination. Henry Kelly, president of the Federation of American Scientists, has asserted that the explosion of a dirty bomb in Manhatten, for example, would lead to nuclear contamination levels similar to those from the meltdown at the Chernobyl Power Plant in the Ukraine (Glanz & Revkin, 2001, p. 4). In addition, the panic and social alarm that would be unleashed by the mere idea of a "nuclear"-based bomb being used would be a great cause for concern to any country.

So-called "dirty" bombs are the result of wrapping conventional explosives with radioactive materials that are more commonly used for industrial or medical applications. John Ashcroft, U.S. Attorney General, admits not only that such bombs are extremely dangerous, but also that Al Qaeda has planned to use such weapons in the U.S.

Whatever their plans for dirty bombs are, it is clear that under Osama bin Laden's guidance, Al Qaeda was working on a program to produce chemical and biological weapons. On a computer disc left behind by bin Laden in Kabul, investigators found documents outlining the precautions necessary before and after the use of chemical, biological, or nuclear weapons. Other documents on the same disc described some experiments carried out with cyanide on rats. According to the information on the disc, another use Al Qaeda had found for cyanide was to combine it with resin and botulism to produce a chemical weapon that could kill 2000 people.

Osama bin Laden once warned in an interview that if the U.S. launched a chemical or nuclear attack against him, they would get one in return. It is also well-documented that bin Laden considered the possession of an atomic weapon by Al Qaeda nothing short of a religious obligation.

It would be easy to dismiss all this as the ravings of a feverish mind. Yet the CIA has published reports warning of the weapons of mass destruction that might be used against the U.S. and it facilities around the world. These weapons would be delivered not by a powerful air force or intercontinental missiles, but rather by suicide bombers, human missiles. It is not a sophisticated method; nevertheless, it is extremely effective. The idea of a young fundamentalist exploding some kind of dirty bomb on 5th Avenue to contaminate the air, water, and food of the whole city has ceased to be the stuff of a fictional screenplay.

A NEW NUCLEAR AGE

FOR THE FIRST TIME IN HISTORY, the U.S. is ready to use its nuclear weapons on a nation that does not possess any, although it possesses other weapons of mass destruction. This changes everything; nuclear weapons are no longer seen as a last-resort threat to persuade, but rather as a combat weapon. Yet the rhetoric turns this fact upon itself. An editorial in the European edition of The Wall Street Journal entitled "Nuclear Posturing" said that the U.S. is talking itself into a new strategy which does not entail deterring the threat of another superpower, but rather attacking any nation or organization that might think of using a nuclear weapon against the U.S. (2002, p.5). Bolstering this frightening new dimension of Realpolitik, the Russian Foreign Minister commented, "There is nothing in the least extraordinary about a nuclear power selecting targets for attack" (cited in: Nuclear posturing, 2002, p. 5).

The rubble of the Twin Towers mixed with the ashes of the

human victims of that tragedy has been cleared away. But something else came crashing down on September Eleventh, namely, the feeling of security, the sense of peace and tranquility that Americans had before. For the first time in a generation, the threat of a nuclear conflict is once again hovering over our heads.

The Bush Administration has been talking about plans to resume nuclear testing. Donald Rumsfeld has insinuated that the U.S. must have its nuclear arsenal ready and available: "Any country that has nuclear weapons has to be concerned of the immense lethality and power of those weapons and has the responsibility to see that they are safe and in order" (cited in: Pincus, 2002, p. 3).

Stephen Schwartz, publisher of the Bulletin of the Atomic Scientists, has commented on Bush's plans, arguing that if the Bush Administration wants to develop new nuclear weapons, than it should be open about it and make the case publicly. Schwartz added that, "If the Bush Administration does not make it public, then perhaps there is something wrong with the policy" (cited in: Pincus, 2002, p. 3).

The reality is that the U.S. officials are playing with the nuclear vocabulary, making sentences and conversations with and about nuclear arms. Just what are the implications of such a game? Robert McNamara, ex-Secretary of Defense feels that apart from breaking the spirit of the non-proliferation treaty that was prolonged in 1995, Bush's apparent willingness to use nuclear weapons is absolutely incredible and ill-conceived. McNamara maintains that such a policy will only serve to exacerbate proliferation of nuclear weapons and cause even more instability (Gardels, 2002, p. 4).

ten:
israel and palestine

The hope for peace and security has given way to disillusion, despair and the murder of civilians. Hatred and cries for revenge have for too long been determining the next step. But there is no path to security and peace other than through dialogue and negotiation.
— Norwegian Foreign Minister Jan Petersen
(2001, p. 6)

THE IMAGES BOMBARD US DAILY now, on television, in newspapers and magazines, pictures of innocent people massacred by a suicide terrorist; images of the terrorists themselves, who appear to be no more than teenagers walking innocently, aimlessly around Jerusalem; small children looking for their toys under the rubble of their home which has just been bulldozed by the Israeli army. This seemingly never-ending chain makes political leaders, analysts, indeed any human who sees it want to cry out: Can justice be revived?

Nobel laureate Jose Saramago (2002) tells a story about how a 16th Century farmer taught a small Tuscan village a lesson. It seems that a rich landowner of the region kept redrawing the lines which delimited the farmer's land, making his holding smaller and smaller until it disappeared altogether. The farmer protested to the landowner, but in vain. He tried to enter a former complaint with the authorities, but it wasn't heard. Finally, outraged and frustrated, the farmer decided to take his dilemma to the villagers themselves.

As in all Italian villages in those days, the Church bell was tolled only at certain hours to call people to mass. It was also rung to mark special occasions, most notably, the death of a villager. Thus, when one day the bell tolled at an odd time and with a slow, melancholic rhythm, the villagers became curious. They hurried to the main square in front of the church to find out who had died. After a few minutes, the ringing stopped and the villagers, now assembled in the square, waited anxiously to see whose passing was to be mourned.

Just then, the farmer came out of the church and stood before the villagers. One of the older townspeople asked him who had died and the farmer answered slowly and clearly, "No one who had a human body died. I tolled the church bell to tell you all that Justice has died in this land" (Saramago, 2002, p. 13).

Unfortunately, most quarrels over land do not end so peacefully. Such problems have existed in the Middle East since time immemorial, but the current conflict stems directly from the events immediately following World War II, when in July, 1947, England divided its colony of Palestine into two separate states. Fifty-five percent of the land was to go to Jewish settlers, many of whom had spent the war years in hiding or in Nazi concentration camps, while forty-five percent of the land went to the Muslim Palestinians.

This partition, which marked the birth of the state of Israel, was approved by the newly founded United Nations. England was relieved to be leaving the zone, European Jewry was happy to see the establishment of a Jewish state, and at least in the eyes of the Western countries, the solution seemed to be good for everyone.

After the departure of the last British soldiers in 1948, however, an army made up of the seven neighboring Arab nations that had refused to sign the approved partition invaded Israel. The objective was clear: to force the 670,000 newly arrived Jewish settlers out of the new state. Apart from the rhetoric of Arab brotherhood, the invading army did not intend to improve the situation of the Palestinians in the area; indeed, aid or shelter for their Muslim brothers has never been particularly forthcoming from the other Arab states. At any rate, the Israelis successfully fought off this invasion, dealing the invaders a severe blow in the bargain. As a result, Israel enlarged its territory from the original 55% to 75% of the former British protectorate. Moreover, 700,000 Palestinians were forced to flee their homes and relocate to the areas not controlled by the Israelis.

In 1949, Israel and the defeated Arab nations signed an armistice. By this truce, Israel was forced to go back to the territories of the original partition with one exception: Jerusalem was to be divided in two. While East Jerusalem continued to be under Jordanian jurisdiction, the Israelis made West Jerusalem their nation's capital, a move that was never accepted or approved by the international community.

Almost two decades later, in 1967, Israel was faced with an imminent attack from Syria, Egypt, and Jordan. Seeing no will to negotiate and feeling that there was no other alternative, the Israelis made a preemptive strike and crushed the would-be invaders. This victory gave Israel not only all of Jerusalem, but also the West Bank, the Gaza Strip, the Sinai Peninsula, and the Golan Heights. These boundaries stood the test of the Yom Kippur War in 1973, and were only changed in 1979, with the U.S.-brokered Camp David Accords, in which Israel signed a peace agreement with Egypt and agreed to return the Sinai Peninsula.

In 1993, after a decade of violence during the Palestinian Intifada, Israel finally got together with the group which claims to best represent the Palestinian people, the PLO (Palestinian Liberation Organization). Just getting the two groups to sit at the table was one of the significant achievements of the Oslo accords; the fact that they were actually able to hammer out some agreements is extraordinary.

These agreements included the PLO's recognition of Israel's "right to exist" as a nation-state. For its part, Israel recognized the PLO as the legitimate representative of the Palestinians. They also agreed to the establishment of a Palestinian government in the West Bank and Gaza. Yasser Arafat, long-time chairman of the PLO, was later elected to head this newly formed government.

But even with these concessions, the pressure from more radical groups on both sides led to continued conflict. Especially disturbing to the Israelis was the fact that terrorist attacks perpetrated by Palestinians went on. Thus, the moderate Israeli leader Ehud Barak was eventually voted out of power to be replaced by the ultimate Israeli hardliner, Ariel Sharon.

According to political analysts, Sharon, known as a ruthless military leader during the decades of conflict between Israel and its neighbors, does not believe in percentages. Rather, he is convinced that the Israelis should be the sole owners of the entire territory of the former British protectorate; thus, he feels absolutely free to send the Israeli army with its heavy artillery and tanks into the Palestinian territories to do as he pleases. Sharon's motives are sometimes cloaked in the rhetoric of strategy, but often it appears to be more of a personal vendetta than any peaceful long-term goal. Indeed, Sharon's lack of remorse basically has the small farmers in the Palestinian settlements as well as the citizens of major Palestinian towns at his mercy, which seems to be in very short supply.

Since 1947, then, the Palestinian people have been losing their land. Right now, with Sharon's crackdown on the latest Intifada, the boundaries of the previously agreed upon Palestinian territory have disappeared completely. And unfortunately for both the Israelis and the Palestinians, rather than peacefully ringing a bell to denounce his people's plight, Yasser Arafat has used bloodshed to air his complaint that Justice has died.

Recently, even European political leaders and analysts – generally sympathetic to the Palestinian cause – have been overtly critical of Arafat and the PLO. They feel that Arafat's objectives have more to do with maintaining his position as the leader of the PLO than with bringing about successful negotiations to obtain territory, peace, and security for the Palestinian people.

In fact, Arafat and his organization, now called the Palestinian Authority, have been deaf to calls from the international community, particularly those countries that give financial aid to the Palestinians, to change his corrupt and dictatorial methods. Disregarding this criticism, instead of instituting changes, Arafat has used the current chaotic situation to put pressure on Israel to end the occupation of the Palestinian territories while simultaneously stifling protests against the Palestinian Authority and its ineffectiveness.

Arafat has assumed the role of the victim to cover up the fact that although he is an autocratic dictator, he is too cowardly to take a stand and make the hard decisions and changes required for peace. Even after the shot in the arm provided by the Oslo agreement, Arafat has neglected to develop the mechanisms that will lead the Palestinians away from a situation of constant conflict to one where organized and democratic institutions can survive and flourish. Indeed, the Palestinian Authority has become an umbrella under which a plethora of security organizations, armed militias, terrorist groups, and Islamic fundamentalists are camouflaged and protected. These groups, with their car bombs and suicide attacks, are not interested in establishing any kind of a democratic system. This, of course, undermines any opportunity for peace and stability in the region, since a democratic political system is one of the essential criteria for Israel to allow the Palestinians self-government. Arafat is thus a key piece of a vicious circle.

Unfortunately, things are not much brighter on the Israeli side of the problem. The international community has repeatedly called on Sharon to exhibit some moderation, which he seems incapable of. The fact that Israel now has control of all the Palestinian territories and absolute military superiority only exacerbates the conflict. Add to this Sharon's uncanny ability both to come up with new obstacles to handing the territories back to the Palestinians and to sell his rationale to the gullible international community, and you have a major roadblock to meaningful negotiations. And this isn't even counting the unconditional support that the U.S. gives Israel.

Currently, Sharon is advocating a return to U.N. resolution 242, made in 1967 after the war with Syria, Jordan, and Egypt, as a ploy to continue moving the boundaries of the Palestinian territories according to his own wishes. And while Arafat may bear much of the blame for the dismal record of the Palestinian Authority, Sharon's demands that this body suddenly transform itself into a democratic, transparent, and accountable institution without allowing any kind of transition time or framework is simply unrealistic. It is also unrealistic for Sharon to demand an end to all violence perpetrated by Palestinians without offering any kind of time-table or structure for turning the territories back over to the Palestinian people. While some may see these demands as idealistic goals, they are actually barricades thrown up to avoid meaningful peace negotiations. In fact, it is doubtful that any changes toward democracy orchestrated by the Palestinians themselves (in the true sense of democracy) would be acceptable to Sharon. In this sense, he is no better than the pre-Oslo PLO in that he simply refuses to acknowledge the right of the Palestinian state to exist.

Under the present circumstances, hope for solutions is scarce.

After years of broken promises and renewed violence, the Palestinian and Israeli leaders have no trust left for each other. They also have little or no desire to talk and negotiate with one another. In fact, it seems that all that remains is bad blood and vengeance.

Despite this, the international community cannot allow the violence to continue, for too many innocent lives are at stake. As hard as it may be to believe, the average Palestinian or Israeli still desires to live peacefully. They call on the world to mediate; a compromise and solution is thus imperative.

Arafat is the linchpin to any deal; the Palestinians will not betray their leader, who has reached almost mythological status among his people, while Sharon and most of the Israelis refuse to trust or work with him. One vehicle toward a possible solution may be to form a type of cosmetic government which would diminish Arafat's relevance among the Palestinians. Or perhaps Arafat could elevate himself to the status of a true martyr by sacrificing his position and cooperating with the international mandate for the sake of his people.

The mandate is already worked out. The parameters for peace established by President Clinton set out the groundwork for a reasonable compromise supported by the international community, which would supervise the evacuation of Israel from the Palestinian territories, the dismantling of controversial settlements, the resettlement of refugees in the Palestinian territories, and any other vital dispute that would arise in this complicated and sensitive process. The U.S. must try to mediate in a less partial manner than in the past, and this may mean disappointing one of its staunchest allies, Israel. But as an editorial in the New York Times pointed out, "Reforms are indeed essential, but the United States must resist Sharon's demand that until they are placed there can be no negotiations on a Palestinian state" (Middle East confusion, 2002, p. 6). The international community, lead by the U.S., must make both the Israelis and the Palestinians accept compromises and make the agreement work.

eleven:
the two sides of the
american face

The true friends of the U.S., those who admire the work done in defense of democratic liberties, are concerned and preoccupied by the way things are changing in the Republic. Their worry is about the U.S.'s inability to live up to its ideals: democracy, justice, openness, respect for human rights, and the commitment to defend the four freedoms of Roosevelt.
— Paul Kennedy (2002, p. 11)

WHATEVER THE UNITED STATES OF America does, it prompts two contrary reactions: admiration and criticism. Because of its prominence in global politics and business, the U.S. is particularly attractive to be judged, sometimes getting credit for the good, but more often receiving the blame for the bad.

For over a decade now the U.S. has been in the position of being the only "superpower." As such, it often succumbs to the temptation of being egocentric and acting unilaterally according to its own needs. Recently, this unilateral behavior has been the major contributing factor to the deterioration of relations between the leaders of the European Union and the U.S. government. The Europeans in general and their leaders in particular feel snubbed by the fact that they are rarely consulted about issues that affect them as well as the U.S. A few of the latest controversial issues have included the steel and iron war, the subsidies for U.S. agriculture, the law allowing U.S. exports through tax havens, and so on. On the political level, the willingness to "go it alone" in any invasion of Iraq has been most disturbing to European leaders. The Americans just don't seem to be taking to heart what European analysts are saying, namely that the best way to address global issues is to act in a multilateral and integrated fashion. For the most part, the Europeans even seem willing to accept U.S. leadership in such international efforts, as long as their views have been seriously taken into consideration.

This begs the question of just what kind of strategy the U.S. will employ to assert its influence internationally now that its hegemony is both evident and overwhelming. The answer is not an easy one.

The government of the U.S. has made a commitment to fight terrorism around the world and to protect both U.S. citizens and U.S. territory. The current administration seems willing to impose drastic measures to achieve this goal, even in the face of the analysts' warning that they should not sacrifice freedom fighting for freedom. According to critics of the Bush administration, this would make the U.S. no better than the enemy it is fighting.

That must not happen, for America's true strength lies in its commitment to civil liberties. Over 100 years ago, in 1899, an article in the Yale Law Journal stated that, "To avoid losing its freedom, [it] must follow the principles of the American Constitution and put the code of law before force, inside and outside of its territory" (cited in: Lamo de Espinosa, 2001, p. 25). This adhesion to law must not be abandoned now.

Several years ago, the editorials in the major European newspapers were predicting the decadence and downfall of the American Empire. Clearly, the U.S. cannot remain the only, unquestioned superpower indefinitely; however, the world is currently witnessing an unprecedented moment of U.S. power:

• The U.S. military is capable of intervening rapidly in any corner of the globe.

• In the case of such an intervention, the U.S. military will not be faced with an equal adversary.

• Even a coalition of armies would not be capable of successfully confronting the U.S. armed forces.

For many, these three points are basically a guarantee that there will be no Third World War in the near future.

Of course, it is possible that there will be local conflicts and wars that, because they do no harm to the U.S. and in some instances may even benefit it, will be allowed, tolerated, or overlooked, as is currently the case in Israel and Palestine. Still, the U.S. should not be complacent, as any local conflict is a "civil world war" that affects everyone in the end, especially the lone superpower.

Whenever one nation has such a lopsided hegemony over the rest, the world is forced into a structure of empire, even though there are various political authorities ostensibly governing the different countries of the globe. The actions of the superpower, however, create ripples felt by all other nations. Thus, in many respects, people around the world are U.S. citizens because they are affected by U.S. policies even though they have no right to vote for those responsible for those policies.

On the one hand, such power is daunting for the rest of the world; on the other hand, as one political commentator remarked, the world should be thankful that the dominant power is concerned about democracy, human rights, and freedom.

Naturally, this power creates an obligation for the U.S. itself, for it is now in a position to use its influence to form a new world order. This world order needs continuity and values that evoke conversion to democratic ideals. In a sense, the U.S. already proved its ability to aid and rebuild nations after WWII. While mistakes and misunderstandings occurred, the U.S. basically left Europe and Japan in better condition that it had found them. America has thus shown that it possesses the wherewithal to help other countries and areas of the world, this time perhaps with more finesse to provoke less resentment.

Without a doubt, one of the national characteristics that has done the most for the U.S. is its particular brand of optimism. This positive attitude has created a dynamic society that generates new technologies, innovative life styles, and a sense of spiritualism radically different from traditional ones. This vision, creativity, and dynamism, coupled with the democratic values so highly prized by the U.S., could become a suitable model to offer the world and to deliver the philosophy of the new world order, with its emphasis on human rights; freedom of worship, assembly, and speech; the right to choose one's own leaders; educational opportunity; equal rights for men and women; pluralism; and the belief that laws can be changed and improved.

The established democracies in the world, including the U.S., should also lend an ear to their young people and put human and environmental issues at least on a par with economic ones. If the International Monetary Fund and the World Bank are allowed to impose their criteria, then the political power of the U.S. will not only be tarnished, but also superceded. Economic considerations are vital to world prosperity and stability, but they should not ride roughshod over all other concerns.

Thus, to maintain the preeminence of their country, U.S. leaders must work together with their allies around the globe to coordinate policies and develop programs to ameliorate and then eradicate hunger, poverty, despair, and hatred around the world. This may include joining forces with other privileged nations to help underdeveloped countries form political, social, and economic structures that will produce stability and sustainable growth for their people. The challenge of the new world order will be to adapt strategies that have been successful in the West to the particular circumstances in other countries. It will not be a quick or easy task.

Despite its critics, though, the U.S. still has its admirers. Its military might is undisputed. Its commitment to democracy and human rights is strong; reports to the contrary are replete with criticism from opposition politicians and American activists, which proves the point that with all its flaws, the U.S. is still a free society. American optimism, often ridiculed as naiveté, is the force behind the most dynamic nation on earth. And although many Europeans are quick to blame the U.S. for the world's ills, there are some who still remember the readiness of the Americans to rebuild Europe. I was told recently of an elderly woman strolling along a Parisian street who was greeted by a young man. Noticing his accent, she asked him if he was American. When he answered that he was, the woman smiled warmly and said, "People don't remember what Americans did for us years ago." Perhaps it was for the U.S.'s own benefit; a healthy ally and trade partner is better than an ailing one. But, like the elderly Parisian woman, many Europeans were thankful to have a generous rather than a vengeful victor.

Yet the U.S. is often guilty of forgetting to cultivate this feeling of goodwill, turning inside itself for solutions rather than trying to establish a consensus among its partners. This was especially true after September Eleventh, when the need to act unilaterally by the U.S. government during the crisis kept affecting the relationship between America and its European allies.

The U.S. went to war against Afghanistan, leaving the Europeans and NATO in the lurch, in spite of having evoked Charter 5 of the alliance for the first time in its fifty year history. The European leaders felt that they had not been given sufficient notice of the U.S.'s actions and that they were out of the loop, even on policy decisions that would ultimately affect them.

Disagreements among political leaders are common enough, but things became a bit more generalized when the "American Letter" was published. This letter, signed by sixty American intellectuals, was meant to defend the Bush administration's policies. It was, however, immediately singled out by Bush's critics, who felt that it neglected to take the U.N. into account on issues of war and peace, leaving the organization responsible only for humanitarian concerns; that is, they should be there to clean up the mess even though they have had no role in making it.

Over a year has passed since the September Eleventh attack. The environment in the U.S. generally seems to be more stable, albeit anxiously guarded. The U.S. border controls are stricter and the regulations for immigrants and those seeking political asylum have been reworded with tougher language. But as security, law, and order became the nation's top priority, fissures began to appear in the Republic, with human rights being the central issue. Critics charge that under the umbrella term of the "War on Terror," the government has curtailed a number of civil liberties, especially of those individuals suspected of aiding, abetting, or being directly involved in terrorism. One particularly thorny issue for human rights advocates is the treatment of prisoners charged with terrorism, but many critics assert that it is all the new policies taken together that contribute to a general loss of the feeling of freedom and security felt by middle-eastern immigrants in the U.S.

Of course, the perception of the loss of freedom may be real whereas the actual loss is not. Be that as it may, it is as important for the current administration to be aware of the five basic precepts their allies use to judge the U.S. These precepts, which in actuality are myths described by historians and political analysts as bits and pieces of President Bush's political philosophy, are:

- That America is governed by a group hard-line executives.
- That the Bush Administration has changed, buried, and

ignored treaties, thus showing disregard for its allies.

• That President Bush supports Israel because of the pressure applied by the Jewish lobby.

• That the American armed forces might intervene in any country at the U.S.'s own discretion to fight terrorism.

• That the triumvirate Bush-Rumsfeld-Cheney have a military "hawk" mentality.

On September 20, 2002, President Bush made public a document entitled "The New U.S. National Security Strategy." This document ushered in the official birth of the president's doctrine. Lionel Barber, a political analyst from the Financial Times, outlined the main points of the doctrine, coining the term "Bushism":

• The war against terrorism has become a top priority for the U.S.'s foreign policy. The supporters will be rewarded, those remaining neutral will be sidelined, and the opponents will be sanctioned, or as in the case of Iraq, attacked.

• The U.S. does not feel obligated to comply with international law, U.N. resolutions, or multilateral regulations that might limit its military endeavors.

• Preemptive attacks are decisive to defend national interests and to stop any threat from materializing.

Barber goes on to assert that the security strategy outlined in the Bush doctrine will be based on an international system, but in a typically American fashion, that is, reflecting the values and national interests of the U.S. (Sahagun, 2002, p. 19).

How exactly will this doctrine be carried out? Within U.S. political circles, the majority of people think that the doctrine needs the backing of the U.N. and the support of a strong international coalition. Only a minority of hard-liners feel that America can go it alone. Thus, while Secretary of State Colin Powell expressed prudence, saying that a coalition will be set up, Defense Secretary Donald Rumsfeld was saying that the U.S. could do it for themselves. Numerous high-profile observers such as ex-Secretary of State Henry

Kissinger, counselor to JFK Arthur Schlesinger, and ex-vice president Al Gore all made blunt statements against the Bush Doctrine, asserting that not only was it bad for the national and international interests of the country, but that it was also illegal and immoral. Ex-president and Nobel peace prize winner Jimmy Carter noted that "the Bush doctrine is a radical break up of traditions that shaped the U.S. political policies under Republican and Democrat presidents for more than fifty years" (cited in: González, 2002, p. 4).

One notable word of advice came from James Baker, ex-Secretary of State with President George Bush the elder, as well as legal counselor to George W. Bush during his election campaign. Baker urged the president to turn to the U.N. to line up a "clear" and "direct" resolution against Iraq (cited in Piquer, 2002, p. 3). Baker, who joined other well-known Republicans Lawrence Eagleburger and Brent Snowcroft on the Iraq issue, echoed Bush's Democrat critics when he stated that the occupation of a country needed the backing of the U.N. and the support of a strong international coalition. In Baker's words, "This would give moral support and political weight to Washington's military initiative" (cited in Piquer, 2002, p. 3). Baker ought to know; it was he who led the last attack on Iraq.

Thus, the American face has two sides; the generous side admired by many, and the scheming side criticized by just as many. Any country probably has these two sides. But it is important to note that it is only in a strong democracy that the criticism can come from within.

twelve:
why do they hate us?

America is not hated for its ideology but for our freedom, our lifestyle, and our products. The more people there are who can't have our products, the more we will be hated. The solution is to share the products with the whole world.
— Micheal Eisner of Disney Inc. (cited in: Carlin, 2001, Viaje… p. 50)

T HE UNITED STATES OF AMERICA HAS always thrived on dynamism, creativity, and productivity. This vitality makes the U.S. a mirror in which many countries view themselves, a mirror in which millions of people see all the things they would like to have and yet have not. Moreover, they see neither the means nor the ways to obtain their wishes in the future.

This disparity of what people see in the mirror and of what they actually have and can ever hope to obtain elicits various, sometimes conflicting emotions and feelings. Along with admiration and amazement come envy, jealousy, and resentment. Many of those looking into the mirror do not even have a glass of drinking water to enjoy. This crude reality stands juxtaposed with the luxury and waste of the American people.

For the most part, Americans are convinced of their essential goodness. They feel sure that the ideals embodied by their nation at its conception are found in them, that they are the most democratic, liberal, and just human beings in the world. Whether this is true or not is not really at issue. The crucial point is that most Americans believe that others view them the way they see themselves and this is definitely not the case.

One problem Americans have is that they are not very good at putting themselves into other people's shoes. Because they neglect to do this, they miss the obvious fact that the view they have of themselves is not shared by the rest of the world. In fact, most Americans are shocked when they learn that people consider them to be arrogant and snobbish because of their lack of interest in learning about other cultures and ways of life.

After George W. Bush was elected – or as some critics put it, "selected" – president in the year 2001, the Spanish newspaper El País ran a story in its Sunday supplement about what the press had considered one of Bush's major gaffes in the campaign, namely his admitted ignorance concerning various world leaders. When the author of the story asked a Denver firefighter if he would support a president who did not know who the leader of the Ukraine was, the man responded, "I don't know either. What has been lost there?" (cited in: Valenzuela, 2001, Why do the Americans…, p. 2).

Unfortunately, this lack of enthusiasm for foreign culture and politics is bolstered by school curricula, which are determined not by the federal government, but by the states and sometimes even more locally by the school districts of each county. Most school systems place little emphasis on subjects such as geography, history, foreign languages, and world cultures. Many political analysts, keen on any point of criticism against the U.S., label this attitude "cultivated ignorance" and argue that it shows just how little interest the average American has for people and circumstances beyond their borders.

That this phenomenon is not considered worrisome to most Americans makes matters even worse. One critic commented that the fact that this cultivated ignorance is seen as comic material for popular television comedians such as Jay Leno and Conan O'Brien show just how arrogant and disdainful the Americans are toward others. As Moises Naim (2002), director of the Journal of Foreign Policy wryly noted, "War is the instrument that God uses to teach geography to North Americans" (p. 6).

The Americans may try to make excuses for their cultivated ignorance, but it will be in vain. Their country possesses some of the world's finest universities and cultural centers. Simply put, they should know better.

If the U.S. were a nation with few pretensions, its citizens' ignorance would probably go unnoticed. But while geography and history are low priorities for local schools, they are incredibly important subjects for a government which has extended its tentacles to every corner of the world and, quite literally, the universe. Many Americans may not know how far-flung their country's power and interests are, but the rest of the world is very much aware of it. And in some ways, the willful ignorance of the Americans causes just as much distrust, resentment, and prejudice as the actions of the U.S. government.

Aware of the bad image the U.S. has in many parts of the world, the Bush Administration announced in 2002 that it will create an office under the direction of Karen Hughes – a longtime political adviser to Mr. Bush – that will be responsible for enhancing America's image overseas. Its mission will be to circulate favorable information about the U.S. in order to change anti-American perceptions and sentiments.

Marketing is all very well and good, of course, but it would perhaps be even more helpful if Americans themselves put some substance behind the publicity. A first step would be to bolster school curricula to include more on world culture, history, and geography. After all, many of today's students are tomorrow's travelers or businessmen; the countries they study now may one day be the subject of their travels or ventures.

The powerful media corporations would do justice both to the countries in which they operate and do business and to the U.S. itself if they broadcast cultural programming about more various countries. The U.S. must realize that it is part of a larger world. Every human being knows what is going on in the United States of America; the rest of the world wants Americans to learn something about them: how they live, how they survive in dire poverty, how they go to bed hungry. They want Americans to learn that they want to have hope for the future, just like most U.S. citizens are privileged to have.

WHY DO THEY CRITICIZE THE U.S.A.?

AFTER THE MILITARY SUCCESS OF THE U.S. armed forces in Afghanistan, the European leaders pleaded with the U.S. government to withstand the temptation of unilateral action and to work together with its allies to create a strong force with which to attack basic issues: disarmament, ecological problems, security, terrorism, and management of the increasingly unmanageable phenomenon of globalization.

Critics and analysts, echoed by European political figures, continued with a vigor even more pronounced than before September Eleventh their condemnation of America's unilateralism, but more concretely they railed against the U.S. government's secretism and lack of communication, which are, of course, the building blocks of unilateral policies. True enough, some observers found the Europeans' "outrage" to be all blather. One political cartoonist took the opportunity to philosophize and criticize simultaneously, having his characters lament the fact that a nation with superior weapon power can impose it's criterion only if it is willing to use the weapons. When one character asks the other if he thinks the Pentagon would use its weapons against the Europeans if they told Bush they did not go along with his policies, the other answers wryly that it would be unlikely, but it is even more unlikely that Europe has any leaders that will actually tell Bush what he should do.

American isolationism is not a new phenomenon. Before the twentieth century, the U.S., perhaps because of its geographic situation, did not generally seek to play a role on the world stage. The unilateralist political philosophy of the current administration, however, differs from historical isolationism in that America is now more than willing to play a major role in world affairs. It simply wishes to do so in its own fashion. This can be seen in many recent policy decisions, made both before and after September Eleventh.

The rejection of the Kyoto Protocol, which sought to address and ameliorate environmental problems; the withdrawal from the 1972 ABM Treaty, which concerned the reduction of missiles capable of carrying nuclear warheads; the refusal to join the ICC or International Criminal Court, even after the Clinton administration had ratified it in 2000; all these are clear indications that the U.S. is determined to go its own way, even at the expense of its partnerships. Add to that the announcement of a new anti-missile project to protect the U.S., along with new tariffs imposed on imported steel, and you have plenty of fuel to feed anti-American sentiment among our allies and the rest of the world.

Not only are the Europeans frustrated by the U.S.'s determination to go it alone, but they also resent being left out of the communication loop. The asymmetrical communication that marks the relationship between Europe and the U.S. makes our allies feel discounted and ignored. Yale University's Paul Kennedy (2002), a critic of Bush and his policies, summed it up by noting that whenever the U.S. armed forces need help rounding up terrorists or gaining access to foreign bases, they expect their allies' full support. If, however, for whatever reason the U.S. does not like some international plan, it withdraws from the coalition without giving any sort of explanation or rationale. Such behavior on the part of the U.S., Kennedy asserts, shows disregard for its allies and its partnerships with them.

That being said, many times European leaders act cynically, trying to please all constituents. It is significant that as the U.S. was about to embark on its war against the Taliban and Al Qaeda, many European countries offered to assist the U.S., but did not specifically call out any military forces to back up that offer. This is clearly an attempt to placate both the U.S. and the anti-war factions in the various European countries.

Critics have seized upon America's military endeavors as proof that 'might makes right' for the U.S.; most analysts see the country's military power as the engine that drives its policies. However, the most important factor driving policy in the past year has been the September Eleventh attacks. The upsurge of caution coming directly from this event has become the standard rationale for allowing policies and accords to fall short of previous commitments.

The idea of world commerce without borders, for example, was issued a severe blow after September Eleventh. Since then, the U.S. has basically blocked the entry of sugar and fruit from the Caribbean countries, which have already begun to feel the repercussions of this move as the only marketable products they produce are forbidden access to their main buyer. There is no other way for these countries to keep their economic development going to improve their standard of living. Another casualty of the attacks was the immigration accord which would have normalized the illegal status of 3.5 million Mexicans currently living in the U.S. Mexican president Vicente Fox was outraged by both the decision to table the agreement and the treatment the U.S. was affording its neighbor: "It seems that the U.S.A does not appreciate enough the partnership condition... it would be good if the U.S., its citizens, and its government recognized that Mexico buys more products and services from the U.S. than Germany, France, Spain, and Italy combined" (cited in Aznarez, 2002, p. 6).

All this occurred just when it seemed that U.S.-Mexican relations were to undergo a heartfelt improvement. Before September Eleventh, Bush had asserted that Mexico was the U.S.'s most important partner. After all that has happened, his statement seems to have been made in another eon.

While America's poorer trading partners may have good reason to resent America's post-September Eleventh policies, some of our wealthier allies have their own agenda. It is significant that between June and September 2002, the most vociferous critics of U.S. policy outside the Middle East have been the Germans, influenced, no doubt, by their large-scale investments in Iraq. As the threat of a U.S.-led attack on Iraq loomed ever larger, German critics became more vitriolic, even asserting that George W. Bush was a greater danger to peace than Sadam Hussein himself. One analyst, after accusing Bush of betraying the fundamental rights of the American system and damaging its democracy, went on to insult the American leaders and called Americans as a whole an "ignorant people" (Tertsch, 2002, p. 3).

Most German critics do not go to such extremes, but a great number seem to think that if the triumvirate Bush-Cheney-Rumsfeld decides to attack Iraq, the aggression will be felt far beyond the conflict between the West and Islam; indeed, they predict that such an act of aggression on the part of the U.S. would trigger a clash of civilizations on either side of the Atlantic. But this is no mere prediction. The critics feel that this conflict between the U.S. and its allies has actually been developing over the entire last year and that it is already causing sensations of distance, repugnance, and cultural abyss. The German critics feel that if this trend continues, the world will become even more unsafe and insecure. The implication underlying their assertions is that Europe will surface as the real peacemaker and gain prestige.

This critique may seem far-fetched, but anti-American sentiment is definitely on the rise in Europe. Of course, the Bush administration has done nothing to play down its role as an instigator; in fact, it fans the flames by providing unconditional support for Ariel Sharon, an unfortunate leader for the Israelis and a ruthless landlord to the Palestinians. Still, to be fair to his critics, Bush's commitment to finding a solution in the area, even with his support for Sharon, has been welcomed by European leaders.

Naturally, it is one thing to welcome a commitment, quite another to agree on concrete action to back it up. In fact, no sooner had they agreed that action must be taken than the European leaders became divided on what for Bush is a main point in any possible solution: the need for new leadership for the Palestinians. Never mind that the Europeans are aware of the corruption rampant in Yassir Arafat's administration, as well as his lack of power to stop it. It is simply very difficult for leaders of that many disparate countries to agree on delicate matters of policy.

Clearly, any political analyst critical of the U.S. – regardless of the specific policy in question – will find ways to blame America for any failure of the negotiations, just as they will be extremely reluctant to praise any successes. Still, if Bush's initiative to restore some modicum of peace to Israel and the Palestinians is at all successful, it will go a long way to lessen the current wave of anti-American sentiment.

But make no mistake. Anti-Americanism is a staple for numerous analysts, political leaders, and intellectuals from Europe, around the world, and even from the U.S. itself. In some way, the anti-American rhetoric is a cover-up for the Le Pens, Haiders, and Roland Freudensteins who are infecting Europe with a new brand of nationalism that is frighteningly similar to the old brand that had Europe in flames for the first half of the twentieth century. But in a more banal sense, anti-American rhetoric is a convenient way to avoid making any real analysis of the evils and deficiencies of those nations whose political figures and analysts continually point the finger at the U.S. This in no way exonerates America, which, as a democracy, should accept criticism when it is due, both from within and without. But it should not be held responsible for all the world's ills, especially when the rest of the world does a good job making mistakes without any help from the U.S.

thirteen:
the u.s.a. versus the
european union

The United States and Europe are the world's only economic superpowers. They are crucial to each other's prosperity and to the stability of the world economy as a whole. They need to start thinking of themselves as an informal "Group of Two" steering committee for the global system rather than as petty antagonists over bananas, steel, and other minutiae.
— Fred Bergsten (2002, p. 8)

IN HIS POLITICAL DIARY, SIR WINSTON Churchill once praised the solidarity that existed between the U.S. and Europe. Expressing his sorrow and condolences for the lives lost at Pearl Harbor, Churchill added that that particular tragedy helped open the eyes of the Americans and their leaders and forced them to look across the Atlantic and see their old friends being massacred by the Nazis. Apparently, witnessing the suffering and death going on in Europe gave Americans pause; they began to realize that they too could fall victim to the evil of Nazism. And so, partly to avoid this and partly to aid their allies, the Americans joined their European allies to defeat Hitler.

Especially since the end of World War II, there has been one overriding common denominator linking the U.S. and Western Europe, namely the cause of freedom. Real conviction exists on both sides of the Atlantic that the basic principles of democracy are worth preserving and fighting for together.

By the same token, both entities are culturally compatible. Moreover, they have extensive economic ties, with Americans having large interests in European countries and the Europeans being major investors in the U.S. Indeed the economic situation of the entire world depends in large part on the prosperity and stability of Europe and North America.

For this reason, the European countries and the U.S. must continue to think in terms of working together with cooperation, coordination, and constancy as their maxims. They must minimize the problems they create for one another and provide progressive and solid leadership to the rest of the world. Specifically in the economic sphere, in which the U.S. and the European Union are the two strong horses pulling the cart of the global economy, the two powers should try to work from a basis of shared fundamentals.

Americans must not be fooled into believing that they alone can dominate the world economy with the same ease with which they control security and military issues. From a historical, cultural, and economic point of view, the U.S.'s logical partner in exercising world leadership in economy and commerce is Europe. Of course, the Americans may contend that since they are both an economic and military superpower, they have no need of Europe, which is merely an economic force. But the U.S. should be aware that such a union would not entail their pulling dead weight around; in the past decade Europe has demonstrated a vital surge of ambition, vigor, and enterprise both in terms of foreign trade and foreign aid. Moreover, in this new era of global interest and global action, international success hinges on alliances. Thus a strong international coalition between the U.S. and the European Union could mark the success of the future.

Such a partnership, however, will require sincere effort. Since the fall of the Soviet Union, the U.S. has neglected its European allies, taking their acceptance of American policies for granted. The alliance between America and Europe is currently in a crucial stage. U.S. leaders must use this historical opportunity to chip away at European distrust which has accumulated over the decades. Viscerally, the Europeans dislike the idea of U.S. hegemony, perhaps because they themselves have seen the last of their colonial glory days. And though many express disdain for the way America physically and culturally occupied their countries after WWII, they also have to admit that there were benefits to be had from enjoying the protection afforded them by the U.S. As political analyst Frank Vendrel (2001) points out, the Europeans should actually be thankful that the American people go along with their country's enormous defense budget. If Europeans had had to foot the bill for the same amount of military might that the U.S. installed in their countries, they would have had to increase taxes and sacrifice many of their highly touted social programs. Thus, to avoid making unpopular tax increases and benefit cuts, the European politicians, rhetoric aside, are often only too willing to allow the U.S. to enforce the proposed solutions for many of the conflicts and troubles around the world.

To be fair to the Europeans, their attitude is not all empty posturing. The scars of WWI are sometimes still visible and the horrors perpetrated and experienced during WWII provide many with an intense anti-war sentiment. As could be seen with the Balkan conflict, the thought of an escalation and spread of local conflicts sends shivers through Europe, whose wounds from the past have yet to be fully healed.

Unfortunately, the pacifist movement in Europe has gone one

step beyond the conviction that military means are not the best way to solve the world's problems; it has evolved into a passivist movement. The Europeans tend to close their eyes and hope that problems will diminish and disappear with time. When they do not, the citizens of Europe are basically expected to grit their teeth and learn to live with them. This attitude creates a general policy of appeasement.

Naturally, the U.S. has and will continue to maintain important relations with many individual European countries. In the word's of David Malowe, a Canadian diplomat, the U.S.'s interactions with its allies consist of an intelligent unilateralism. Malowe finds that part of the reason for this stance is that the U.S. "knows what it wants" whereas Europe is still trying to "find itself" (cited in: Ortega, 2001, p. 4).

This state of affairs may not last much longer. The importance of the European countries, now more strongly united than ever within the European Union, is increasing steadily. Their union gives them a new strength, allowing them the opportunity to consolidate their influence as a united body. Although the dream of a federalized "United Europe" may be decades in the making, there is an increasing tendency toward more concerted action in the political and military sphere. Economically, the Europeans have made astounding progress, creating an enormous free trade zone, a dynamic single market, and a strong single currency. As William Pfaff (2001) points out, "Along with these strides to form a strong economic Europe have come protectionist Europe, subsidized Europe, cultural exception Europe, social protection Europe, socialized medicine Europe, antitrust Europe, anti-dumping Europe, and to a certain extent, anti-globalization and anti-American Europe"(p. 3). All these different aspects of Europe, for better or for worse, are currently thriving.

Even so, the European Union was caught empty handed when the tragedy of September Eleventh struck, with nothing to offer their oft-resented protector but moral support. Since then, the European nations have approved the formation of a rapid reaction force, whose main objectives include peace keeping, crisis management, and humanitarian efforts. They have also made several new agreements with the U.S. that involve the sharing of intelligence, tracking of financial assets of terrorist organizations, and cooperation in both judicial and law enforcement issues.

While the European Union and the U.S. were trying to hammer out ways to work together, the North Atlantic Treaty Organization (NATO) launched into concerted action, activating Article Five of its charter for the first time in its fifty-three year history. This article calls on NATO members to come to the aid of a member who has suffered an aggression. As the organization that manages the political and military influence of the U.S. in Europe, both with its allies and with those outside of the alliance, NATO has been an essential organization for Washington. It proved its post-Cold War validity in its successful effort to cut the Balkan crisis short. Working, then, within the alliance frameworks of the European Union (E.U.) and NATO, the U.S. can successfully manage its relations with Europe in order to present a more united front to the new threats around the globe. That being said, the U.S. should not take its ties with the E.U. and NATO for granted. The latter organization has problems which must be solved so that it can fulfill its potential as the military and political engine for the 21st Century.

Such an engine is desperately needed in a world with powder kegs at every turn. Numerous heavily armed guerilla and terrorist groups, governments that reward suicide terrorists for killing innocent civilians, Islamic fundamentalist terrorist cells cruising through European neighborhoods as an army of radical suicide bombers, the ever-increasing proliferation of weapons of mass destruction – this is the current world situation. In the midst of this kind of chaos, two world powers like the U.S. and the European Union cannot afford to act like jealous siblings, bickering over issues of pride.

On the European side, the anti-American rhetoric is on the upswing, as politicians blame the U.S. for being everything from unilateral to arrogant, from having bad manners to oversimplifying complex issues. Even the sparse praise they can offer comes with disclaimers. Thus, when Chris Paten, the E.U. foreign affairs commissar, commended the U.S.'s success in Afghanistan, saying that it demonstrated both American ability and American intelligence, he was quick to add that the victory may reinforce the dangerous attitude that the use of military power alone is the only way to guarantee security.

French foreign minister Hubert Vedrine was more personal with his remarks, calling President Bush "simplistic." But whether these remarks are heartfelt or not, they reflect what Spanish Prime Minister told President Bush at a recent meeting between the two, namely that to gain popularity in Europe nowadays, "The best way to do it is to criticize the U.S." (cited in: Richburg, 2002, p. 17).

This name-calling and bickering would almost be funny were it not for the fact that it influences important policy decisions. Thus, while U.S. Secretary of State Colin Powell, annoyed by the comments of both Paten and Vedrine, emphasized that the U.S. would not sacrifice its interests to play to the crowd with multilateral policies (Yarnoz, 2002, The E.U. condemns... , p. 5), Javier Solana, the chief foreign policy emissary for NATO pleaded that the rhetoric be toned down on both sides. Solana underscored the importance of mutual respect in a relationship that "is too serious to gamble with" (cited in: Erlanger, 2002, p. 17). Indeed, the cooperation between the U.S. and Europe is as necessary today as it has ever been.

Unfortunately, the relationship is strained, at best. The U.S., vested with overwhelming military superiority, feels that it has a historical opportunity – indeed, an obligation – to act, even if it means acting alone. This conviction was expressed by President Bush when he said, "History has given us the opportunity to defend freedom and fight tyranny and that is exactly what we are doing. We will not let our guard down" (cited in: Yarnoz, 2002, The E.U. condemns..., p. 5).

Most European leaders and some leaders of the opposition in the U.S. disagree. As Senator Patrick Leahy stated, "We can't begin a war to defend our values and give them up at the same time" (cited in: Ramonet, 2002, p. 6). The Europeans are loath to be dragged into a conflict which is seen as protecting mostly American interests, hence the resistance to go along with the current warlike atmosphere in Washington.

This all contributes to the fact that maintaining the brief flurry of cooperation that occurred after September Eleventh is becoming more complicated. As Schnabel Rockwell, U.S. ambassador to the E.U., remarked, "With the European Union taking more initiative on its own, it is more difficult to work as associates" (cited in: Yarnoz, 2002, Europe resists..., p. 4).

Non-diplomats put it even more bluntly. Robert Kagan, an American intellectual and political analyst, predicts that the most significant change to be brought about by September Eleventh will be the break up of the alliance between the U.S. and Western Europe (Kapuscinski, 2002, La globalización..., p. 9). Throughout the last half of the twentieth century, first the fight against fascism, then the Cold War kept the U.S. and Western Europe together. Today, without the common enemy of Nazism or Communism, the U.S. and the ever-stronger European Union find that their different views of the world make it difficult for them to walk the same path. The various tacks taken in response to the threat of global terrorism may bring about some superficial cooperation, but the ideological rift will probably widen. While the U.S. government views the disorder and anarchy that abide in the rest of the world as the product of the machinations of a mortal enemy, Europe is less convinced. Thus, whereas the U.S. sees the only valid response to be one of force to defeat the enemy with firepower, the Europeans, burned by half a century of armed conflict, envision the road to peace through negotiations, compromise, appeasement, and exchange of ideas. With such different concepts, it seems unlikely that the U.S. and Europe will be able to find a common ground on which to work together.

Commenting on the current situation, the director of Le Monde Diplomatique, Ignacio Ramonet (2002), states that the reason for the rupture is the fact that Washington believes that it has unlimited power and the right to use it. This, along with a general feeling of moral superiority, makes Americans feel that they can declare other governments or countries "Enemies of Humanity" by their own criteria and expect others to go along with it. Thus, since the U.S. attacked Iraq, every other country in the world either has to accept this or risk being branded as friendly to terrorist organizations or supporters of terrorism.

This all or nothing rhetoric is counterproductive. The world cannot afford to lose faith and the leaders of the U.S. and Europe must not fall into extremist and radical responses, but rather prudent and moderate solutions. Churchill was optimistic in his day, saying that although Americans make mistakes, at the time for resolution, they find the right answer. The Americans should be more open to dialogue and the Europeans should be less critical; only then can the democracies of the world hope to find answers to global problems.

fourteen: the u.n. – an illusory powerhouse?

SOON AFTER SEPTEMBER ELEVENTH, THE world was flooded with many different theories on the best way to fight international terrorism. War became an option.

In the days and weeks after the tragedy, as people became aware of America's vulnerability, national security and safety took center stage. Indeed, these two concerns became justifications for war against what were seen as the hordes of radical and militant fundamentalists from all over the world who were being trained specifically to hurt not only American citizens in their own country or abroad, but also anything that could be roughly construed as being American or part of what the U.S. stands for.

Still, a U.S.-led war was not the only option discussed. One alternative that was taken to heart by various analysts was the establishment of a special U.N. commission, set up by the U.N.'s 190 members and comprised of various countries from different regions of the world. This special commission, modeled after the post-war tribunals at Nuremberg and Tokyo, would be subject to the authority of a renewed and revitalized U.N. organization and would be vested with the authority to investigate, apprehend, and bring to justice the perpetrators of terrorist acts as well as those individuals, organizations, and governments who support and feed them. To this end, this hypothetical commission would thus have the power to impose economic, political, and military sanctions as dictated by an international mandate.

Those who proposed this option hoped that such a system would become the foundation of a method of punishment that the whole world would approve of. It was hoped that this type of commission would be the means to empower the multilateral structure already in existence and that it would lead to the formation of a responsible, democratic, and international world order.

The U.S. Government chose the war option, as pressure to uproot the foundations of terror organizations quickly and completely bore down heavily on U.S. leaders. Thus, President George W. Bush and his team, endowed with the strongest military power in the history of the world, opted to ignore the U.N. Security Council's authority on matters of war and peace. This choice was reinforced a year later when the government published a document entitled "The New U.S. National Security Strategy," which clearly placed the U.S. above the international U.N. mandate. This attitude made manifest President Bush's decision to simply overlook the Security Council's configuration, which was designed even before the end of WWII to confront violators of U.N. objectives.

At the end of the Gulf War in April 1991, the U.N. Security Council approved Resolution 687, which set the terms for the ceasefire between Iraq and the Allied nations, among them the U.S., England, France, and Kuwait. The same resolution also mandated the disarmament of Iraq along with the actual destruction of its weapons of mass destruction.

In October 1998, seven years after the approval of Resolution 687, the Iraqi government stopped cooperating with the U.N. weapons inspectors (UNSCOM), accusing them of spying for the U.S. and Russia. By the end of the year, the 140 inspectors charged with verifying Iraq's compliance with the U.N. resolution left the country. Even U.N. General Secretary Kofi Annan had to acknowledge that the UNSCOM commission was discredited by this act.

Four years passed, and as the spotlight shifted to other parts of the globe, Iraq's dictatorial leader remained the same defiant man he always was. In fact, it was argued that Saddam Hussein had become even more dangerous and aggressive. This was especially worrisome as the tension in the Middle East became increasingly explosive.

What did the world say to the situation in Iraq in the years leading up to the second War in the Gulf? The French said little, but then again, they had a large part in creating the situation in the first place. The Germans also played down the danger of allowing Saddam to stay in power, but of course they could not afford to be accused of instigating a second Holocaust. The U.S. pledged unconditional support to the state of Israel, no matter what the course of its leaders. Where was the U.N. Security Council in all of this?

On September Eleventh, Al Qaeda and the Taliban of Afghanistan changed the rules that had governed the world since the end of the Second World War. President Bush became intolerant and threatened to make a preemptive strike against Iraq as a way "to cope with terrorist threats and the dangers posed by the spread of nuclear, biological, and chemical arms" (Gordon, 2003, p. 1). The President's doctrine was criticized by his close advisors, his friends, the Democrats, and European leaders alike because it excluded the allies and the U.N. Security Council.

Moved by this criticism, President Bush went to the U.N. Headquarters in New York to give its members and the rest of the world a history lesson. In his speech, Bush made clear that Iraq was clearly a threat not only to the U.S., but to the entire world community, saying:

The United Nations Organization was born with the hope that helped survive a World War, the hope that the world would move toward justice and escape the old patrons of trouble and fear. The founding members decided that world peace would never be destroyed again be the will and evilness of any man...

The behavior of the Iraqi regime is a threat to the U.N. and to peace. Iraq has answered dozens of demands from the U.N. with dozens of provocations. Everyone is on trial and the U.N. is in the midst of a difficult and decisive moment....

Will the resolutions of the security council be applied and accomplished or will they be put aside without consequences? Will the U.N. serve the founders' objectives or will it be irrelevant? (Cited in: Kennedy, 2002, p. 14)

On November 8, 2002, President Bush got the answer to his questions.

Resolution 1441 was unanimously approved by the fifteen members of the Security Council, the five permanent members with veto rights, namely the U.S., Russia, China, France, and England, and the ten rotating members at the time, namely Bulgaria, Camaroon, Chile, Guinea, Spain, Angola, Mexico, Germany, Pakistan, and Syria. As one British journalist noted, the new resolution gave "the U.N. inspectors (UNMOVIC or the U.N. Monitoring Verification and Inspection Commission) sweeping authority to hunt down Iraq's outlawed weapons programmes and [demanded] that Iraq cooperate to the full" (Usborne, 2002, p. 1).

Hans Blix, the man chosen to head the UNMOVIC operation

in Iraq, gave his first report on the inspectors' findings on January 27, 2003, forty-five days after the inspections were restarted on November 2, 2002. To put it succinctly, Blix found that Iraq needed to provide substance. In his words, the fact that the Iraqis did not hinder the inspectors was not enough to fulfill the U.N. mandate; the Iraqis needed to cooperate actively, which they did not do.

The problems involved in the weapons inspections and the resulting war that left the Western world divided begs the question: Is the power of the U.N. Security Council illusory or real?

Lakhadar Brahimi, the so-called U.N. "wizard" in Afghanistan recently defined the U.N. in general and his job in particular:

> It is strange being a U.N. superstar. Your job is to take on the world's most intractable injustices and you presume to speak for all the world's people, yet your power is to a large extent illusory. You have no money, no armies, and your once proud New York headquarters are crumbling. It is not a robust mechanism, but it is the best we have. (cited in Mallaby, 2003, p. 8)

As WWII was drawing to a close in 1945, American and British authorities looked on the failure of the League of Nations with shame and anger. This organization, formed with such a sense of purpose after WWI, had not been able to stop the powerful nations from intimidating and conquering their neighbors, which directly led to the atrocities of the 1930's and the ensuing war. In view of this enormous failure, American leaders and their British counterparts decided to create a new organization with not only a robust leadership and a strong structure, but also with well-defined objectives and clear goals. Protecting the interests of the victorious nations after the war was, of course, one of the foremost aims of that structure.

This last point had been a hallmark of the U.N.'s precursor as well. The League of Nations had been created as an experiment by the French and the Russians after the First World War, mainly to protect the interests of the five victors of that conflict. In contrast to the U.N, however, the League of Nations was plagued with a weak structure and poor leadership. Ironically, it was too democratic and deliberative. Its greatest weakness, though, was that several of the world's most powerful nations were not members of the League; the U.S., for example, never joined while Japan, Germany, Italy, and the Soviet Union either left or were expelled during the political crises that engulfed these nations in the 1930s.

When the U.N. was formed after WWII, its basis was composed of a nucleus of the five victors of that conflict: the United Kingdom, the U.S., the USSR, France, and China. These nations became the five permanent members of the U.N. Security council and were given the veto privilege. This privilege, hotly contested by the smaller nations, was introduced to keep the powerful nations within the structure of the U.N. It was thought that with this privilege, the most powerful countries would not leave the organization under the pretext that their interests were not being safeguarded. With this foundation, then, the U.N. became a truly international organization with a powerful and more or less efficient system that endowed it with the capability to confront any nation or organization that violated its objectives.

The U.N. charter was written up in San Francisco, California, in 1945, and was signed by fifty nations, including the five permanent Security Council members. The U.N. currently boasts 190 members, with several other entities involved as observers (e.g. the Vatican and the Palestinians).

In the early days of the organization, the Security Council could not authorize resolutions without a unanimous vote. In addition, a single veto from one of the five permanent members was enough to block any resolution, even if it had been approved by the rest. Thus, every effort to create peace through international agreements or to use collective force depended on the unanimity of the five permanent members of the Security Council. As mentioned before, although no official rationalization of the veto privilege was ever given, the individuals and nations involved in founding the U.N. strongly believed that without such a rule, the organization would have never found support among the more powerful countries.

In any case, noble as its cause and objectives were, two factors seriously hampered the effectiveness of the U.N.: the Cold War and the end of European colonialism. The former arose from the post-war situation in Europe, which had been divided into an Eastern Block, dominated by the Soviet Union and the Western Block, which, dominated by the U.S., also included two of the other victors, Great Britain and France. After the Communist revolution in China, that enormous country put its weight on the Eastern side of the scale. Thus, the five permanent members of the Security Council were pitted against each other. By breaking the cohesiveness of the Security Council, the Cold War seriously – almost fatally – reduced the usefulness of the U.N., as each side vetoed the resolutions proposed by the opposing side. As for the break up of the former European colonies in the Southern Hemisphere, these new countries found that unfortunately, independence did not tend to ameliorate their poverty, lack of development, border conflicts, internal divisions, or civil strife.

Gradually, however, the original objective of the U.N., which as one American analyst has put it was to "dissuade and defeat the evil ones" (Kennedy, 2002, 14), was replaced with chores never imagined by its founders. These included regulating commerce, supervising developmental assistance, assessing human rights situations, and distributing food to famished and war-torn countries.

In the months leading up to the second Gulf War, though, President Bush called for a return to what he held to be the primary goal of the organization. The question then became: would the U.S. abide by the Security Council's resolutions on the critical issue of war with Iraq?

The Bush Administration openly stated that it would welcome the support of the U.N. and the Security Council, but it simultaneously put the world on notice. In the words of Secretary of State Colin Powell, "We continue to reserve our sovereign right to take military action against Iraq alone or in a coalition of the willing." Was a new "Cold War" on the horizon?

Two Western allies and permanent members of the Security Council – France and the U.S. – seemed to be on a head-on collision course. Both countries had the power of the veto to annul the other's proposals concerning Iraq. Would France, once saved from defeat and humiliation by the U.S., break its traditional alliance? Were the interests of ELF and the other French corporations who have been the beneficiaries of France's relationship with Iraq sufficient to override their country's relationship with the last superpower and possibly prompt a historical break?

France was not the only Western nation which opposed the Bush policy. With Germany stating that it would not support a war against Iraq, was the U.S. facing a possible split within NATO, or even an end to that organization?

Ironically, President Bush never seemed to be perturbed or even overly concerned about the opposition coming from Germany's Foreign Minister Joschka Fischer or that from his French counterpart Dominique Villepin. Even when Javier Solana, the former top man at NATO who is now the Foreign Minister for the European Union, offered his criticism, the Administration was unmoved. In his State of the Union address on January 28, 2003, President Bush reiterated his belief that "the destiny of the U.S. does not depend on somebody else's decisions" (Gonzalez, 2003, p. 2).

In fact, in that speech, President Bush implied that the UNMOVIC inspectors, along with the IAEO (International Atomic Energy Organization) inspectors, simply did not have a chance since Hussein's regime was not willing to cooperate and help them. In fact, most people in the Bush camp felt that Saddam Hussein had already rejected his last opportunity to disarm, which showed his disregard for the U.N. in particular and the world in general (Gonzalez, 2003, p. 2).

In the end, the U.N. was unable to prevent a war in Iraq. The question then became: will it be able to prevent a similar conflict from erupting if the Bush Administration decides to bear down on North Korea as well? The only way it could do this would be to stop North Korea from continuing with its nuclear weapons program. The U.N. was not successful getting Saddam to disarm; will it be more adept with this new situation?

Time will tell.

fifteen:
public opinion –
superpower

It would be pleasant to report that the soldiers and officers of the 8th Army have identified their role in the global strategy against Communism. But there is little evidence of any such understanding. Few of the soldiers seem able to identify themselves with any national goal.
— "1953 Frustrated by Korean War" (2003, p. 10)

FEBRUARY SIXTEENTH AND SEVENTEENTH OF the year 2003 marked the beginning of the world's crusade for peace. Millions of people marched through the streets of thousands of cities chanting slogans against the war and carrying posters, banners and signs reading, "No to this war," "Don't attack Iraq," "No blood for oil," "Throw Bush out before throwing bombs," and "Bush the butcher." People protested against the war in Iraq, against the preemptive war doctrine, and also against the destruction of the present international judicial system, namely the U.N. Security Council. Political credibility reached a new low and the thus discredited politicians gave way to a new superpower: public opinion.

Public opinion, the whispering builder of societies, communities, cultures, and religions was given new life through television and internet. One editorial in the New York Times affirmed that, "Public Opinion has begun to be written with capital letters" (cited in: Verdu, 2003, p. 8).

Public opinion is a free, democratic institution; it speaks from a more ethical perspective than politicians do. Public opinion is the true expression of a healthy heart because it is more human that elected leaders and more truthful than public institutions. It is a voice that elected officials cannot afford to ignore.

While television screens display the sounds and horrors of war, computers are heating up with pulses from e-mail, chat groups, and web pages, all clamoring to keep the flame of peace burning and alive. The internet has been the fundamental instrument in the creation of this global movement for peace, assisted by U.S. expertise. The most prominent web sites to invite people to demonstrate against this war have all come out of the U.S.: www.moveon.org, with more than 700.000 members, www.peace-action.org, www.winwithoutwarus.org, www.truemajority.org, and www.endthewar.org, to name the five most important sites. These groups have provided protesters with critical information, such as the locations and names of the organizers of mass demonstrations, as well as the various transportation options of how best to get to them. No details have been left out.

Peter Scurman, the executive director of Move On said, "It gives people the opportunity to be heard, especially when the separation between public opinion and government officials is so great" (cited in: Fresneda, 2003, p. 20). Furthermore, the organizers of the web page "United for Peace and Justice" published an open letter addressed to their 'brothers and sisters' of the world to remind the global community that "President Bush does not speak in their names. The people of the U.S. do not have anything to gain in this war" (cited in: Verdu, 2003, p. 8).

The web page "Books not Bombs," jointly organized by a number of universities, has urged students to go on strike to protest against the war in Iraq. The "United Association for Peace and Justice" web page organized emergency acts from coast to coast the day the war was launched.

Public opinion, strong as it is, did not manage to stop the war, which began on March 20, 2003. Still, public opinion has done much in the way of shaping how the first war of the twenty-first century will be remembered, namely as an unwanted war, one not authorized by the U.N. Security Council, and unnecessary for saving the world. Of course, this war will mostly be remembered by the families and friends of the American and British soldiers who die fighting it and especially by the Iraqi people, whose suffering is impossible to describe fully.

THE IRRATIONAL WISDOM OF THE WAR

IN 1815, ANDREW JACKSON DEFEATED the British in what was to be their last invasion of the U.S. Since then, the Americans have felt invulnerable on their own continent, even despite the bombing of Pearl Harbor. In fact, this precious dream of the American Fortress lasted for nearly 200 years, when it ended tragically with the events of September Eleventh, 2001.

The terrorist attacks of that fateful date pushed security and safety to the top of the Bush Administration's list of priorities. Frank Bruni, George W. Bush's autobiographer, wrote that "the obsession to build a more secure world reigns in the White House and President Bush is convinced that an intervention in Iraq will contribute to reaching this objective" (cited in: González, 2003, La hora..., p. 2).

The Bush Administration made many allegations justifying its antagonism toward Iraq. Those accusing Saddam Hussein of producing weapons of mass destruction were supported by revelations made by an Iraqi defector and civil engineer, Adnan Ihsan Saeed Haidery, who allegedly helped rebuild Iraq's facilities to produce such weapons after the first Gulf War. Francis Brooke, a consultant to the Iraqi National Congress, reacted to these revelations by calling for the overthrow of Saddam as a direct threat to the U.S.

Senate Majority Leader, Thomas Daschle, D-South Dakota, did not agree with this assessment, asserting that, "A strike against Iraq at this time would cause serious problems in the Middle East and give the Islamic world concerns about U.S. policy" (cited in: Sipress & Slevin, 2001, p. 1). An analyst writing for the International Herald Tribune agreed, adding that "Attacking another country just to change its regime is a grave matter and will affect the international rules and will have legal implications" (Malley, 2003, p. 8).

This war, however, did not arise suddenly, a fact which adds to the impression that it was a war of choice, not necessity. Indeed, the issue of what to do with Iraq was already a topic in President Bush's first State of the Union address, when the President brought to the attention of the American people the existence of what he deemed the "Axis of Evil Nations": Iraq, Iran, and North Korea. According to one commentator, during that speech, the President "gave the impression of using his words to launch a sustained effort for the U.S. Forces in helping Saddam Hussein's foes topple the Iraqi dictator" (Hoagland, 2002, p. 1).

This obsession with Iraq was given a shot in the arm with the proclamation of the Administration's preemptive war doctrine. This flew in the face of all conventional thinking, with international lawyers and legal representatives from the U.N. all contending that this new doctrine of preemptive strikes against perceived threats did not conform with Chapter Seven of the U.N. Charter, which only recognizes the right of individual or collective self-defense.

With this in mind, and perhaps also thinking of the resistance such a scheme would arouse in Senator Daschle and other respected U.S. statesmen, including several Republicans and ex-President Jimmy Carter, President Bush decided to initiate a different strategy, namely demanding the return of U.N. weapons inspectors to Iraq. Bush's speech at the U.N. regarding the necessity to keep Saddam Hussein in check was convincing enough to prompt the adoption of Resolution 1441, which was basically a reaffirmation of previous resolutions designed to disarm Iraq.

Most likely, Bush hoped that Saddam would not comply with the new resolution, since any refusal to welcome U.N. inspectors would indeed be proof that Iraq was in the business of producing weapons of mass destruction. He was not the only political figure to espouse this view; Dame Margaret Thatcher, former prime minister of Britain remarked, "Saddam Hussein will never comply with the conditions we demand of him. His aim is in fact quite clear: to develop weapons of mass destruction" (Thatcher, 2002, p. 8).

The sequence of events has since shown that the weapons of mass destruction were not the U.S. Administration's main concern; what President Bush was really talking about was the need for a regime change in Baghdad. The talk of weapons of mass destruction came later, as an additional justification of the real issue.

In fact, the justification was badly needed, for Bush's idea of toppling Saddam Hussein was not readily accepted by France, Germany, and Russia, all known beneficiaries of the lucrative business agreements carried out with Saddam, his cronies, and his regime. President Chirac of France, and Germany's Chancellor Schroeder became openly critical of the Bush Administration's unilateral ambitions. They argued that the U.S. government was just trying to demonstrate its hegemony rather than deal with Saddam's brutal tyranny over the Iraqi people. However, apart from an obvious demonstration of American military might, political analysts cited other equally important underlying motivations for Bush's insistence that Saddam Hussein be overthrown, for example, the desire of the U.S. to control, at least temporarily, 17% of the world's oil reserves, as well as the control of the water rights from Iraq's main rivers, the Tigris and the Euphrates. Similarly, the U.S. felt a need to establish its military more firmly in the Middle East, largely out of concern for its major ally there, Israel.

The French, Germans, and Russians, also driven by pragmatic interests, were determined to undermine Bush's efforts to use a U.N. Security Council-sanctioned war to oust Saddam. Their ventures in diplomacy, however, crashed against the unilateral determination of President Bush, which was, of course, bolstered constantly by his hawkish advisors: Vice President Dick Cheney, Secretary of Defense Donald Rumsfeld, National Security Advisor Condoleeza Rice, and analysts Paul Wolfowitz and Richard Perle. Even the more moderate Secretary of State, Colin Powell, supported war as a means to an end.

Meanwhile, the lack of clear results from the U.N. inspectors in charge of verifying the conditions stated in Resolution 1441 gave the U.S. and Britain the impetus to try and push a new resolution through the Security Council, one that would specifically authorize a war against a non-compliant Iraq. This effort succumbed to diplomatic blundering. As commentator William Pfaff noted, "A final U.N. resolution and vote were abandoned by the allies not only because they lack the votes for authorizing war, but also because they face the possibility of a majority vote against them – sending them to war in actual defiance of the Security Council" (2003, Diplomatic blunders..., p. 8).

Not only did the poor diplomacy on both sides do nothing to form a consensus on what to do about Iraq, its aftershocks rocked the world, causing several unfortunate casualties:

• Resultion 1441 was torn to shreds.

• The U.N. Security Council was brought to its knees in a fashion reminiscent of the Cold War era.

• Fissures within NATO not only became more visible, they

threatened to render the Atlantic Alliance powerless.

• The veneer of unity the Europeans had worn since the birth of the Euro was absolutely lost,

• And worst of all, the war against Iraq began on March 20, 2003, a war conducted by the U.S. and Britain without even the tacit support of the U.N.

When this immediate crisis ends and the bickering begins over who should get the juiciest contracts to rebuild a bombed-out Iraq, the U.S. should bear in mind all that has been destroyed in its dogged fight to topple Saddam. And if Americans really want to make the world a safer place, they should work as much on diplomacy as on military strategy and start exporting their hopes rather than their fears.

sixteen:
globalization

*This is globalization in process. As traditional boundaries
tumble down, as peoples and nations reach further, faster
and deeper into other peoples and other nations, we are
becoming a soup of culture, politics, society, race and language
sloshed into a large melting pot labeled humanity.*
— Rachel Leow (2002, p. 9)

DISTANCES HAVE BEEN SHORTENED, high-tech
communication makes people feel closer. Exchange of information has been made easier than ever before. Human beings
from different parts of the world now depend on one another. We
are becoming a global village where all will live with respect and
dignity. This is the idealistic side of globalization, but the reality is
quite different. There are less who have a lot and more who have
nothing. If this is globalization, who really wants it?

Globalization offers numerous possibilities and opportunities
to humanity, including improvements in communications, exchange

of information, education, and much more. But this potential relies on the existence of chains of interdependency which reach every corner of the world.

The term globalization is used all the time these days and yet it seems premature to speak of a global society, a global culture, and a global political system. Perhaps the closest we have come so far is in our attempt to establish a global system of justice in the form of the International Criminal Court (ICC). Established on July 1, 2002, with sixty countries affiliated, the Court immediately became a symbol of the U.S.'s unilateral philosophy when President Bush refused to accept the court's jurisdiction for U.S. citizens. This was a heavy blow to the fledgling organization, especially since the U.S. had signed the status of its approval of the court four years before in Rome.

In the economic sphere, globalization is the trend as well, especially with the perception that the combination of free market economy and democracy has enjoyed great economic and political success in the Western nations. The globalization establishment predicts that this success will spread to the rest of the planet to make it better and more balanced. Nevertheless, social science analysts assert that these hypothetical predictions are totally speculative since "no people and no nation can truly prosper unless the bounty of a collective ingenuity and opportunities are available and accessible to all" (Davis, 2002, p. 8).

This assertion that the globalization movement is uncontrollable is a source of concern. The rules so far have created great disparities and problems. In the words of Harvard sociologist Daniel Bell, "Outside of major industrial nations, globalization has not brought integration and harmony, but rather a firestorm of change that has swept away languages, cultures, ancient skills and visionary wisdom" (cited in: Davis, 2002, p. 8).

The lack of controls in the financial markets, the strong tendency toward monopolies, the greed of multinational corporations and the bold objectives of profitability at all costs have been shocking to poor communities. These are the most obvious drawbacks of globalization. If these problems are coupled with the lack of sensitivity and concern of corporations and autocratic officials for both human rights and ecological issues, the consequences are obviously undesirable.

Changing the current course of the globalization phenomenon is not going to be easy; nevertheless, the rich nations, including the U.S., the European Union, and Japan, must help the poorer nations develop the necessary infrastructures to address their staggering problems. The privileged people of the world must help eliminate hunger. They must help the developing world initiate ways by which their people would have the means to live with dignity. They must see to it that the Third World improves its human rights record by establishing a system of justice which upholds equality, freedom, and the rule of law, as put into words fifty years ago in the Universal Declaration of Human Rights. This is perhaps the most important goal of all, for as Nobel Prize winner José Saramago (2002) of Portugal wrote, "Without justice based on human rights, the mouse of human rights will be eaten by the cat of the economic globalization" (p. 13).

These changes are no longer an option for the wealthier nations. As Bell points out:

> The voices of the poor who deal each moment with the consequences of the environmental degradation, political corruption, overpopulation, the gross distortion in the distribution of wealth and the consumption of resources, who share few of the material benefits of modernity, will no longer be silent. (cited in Davis, 2002, p. 8)

The chain of global dependencies has left the doors wide open for the ferocious neoliberalism that unscrupulously invaded both the industrialized and the developing world. The neoliberal socioeconomic philosophy, bolstered by its three central ideas of deregulation, privatization, and liberalism, has impaired the economy of many of the poorer nations. Not only has it taken away the ability to fight free-enterprise, it has also removed the price controls for agricultural products such as coffee, bananas, etc. The result has been that many countries that depend solely on these types of agricultural goods for their survival are now utterly unable to control their own destiny, provide basic human services to their citizens, and improve their standard of living.

Another aggressive predator is so-called "naked capitalism." Under the protective umbrella of globalization and with the support of the new technology, naked capitalism incites the flow of new capital into the industrial and agricultural markets of countries with autocratic governments controlled by corrupt officials and the privileged clans that manipulate the countries' economies for their own personal gain and dictatorial power.

The exclusion of the disadvantaged from this process creates enormous disparities between the poor, who are in the majority, and the rich, who are a very small minority indeed. South America, Africa, and Southeast Asia are regions with numerous examples of such governments and economic systems.

But why should the industrialized world care about such things? Apart from any deeper moral or ethical issues, there is one very pragmatic, almost egotistical reason for the developed world to take note, namely that economic disparities are a well-known cause of social and political unrest as well as full-blown wars. They are also a root cause for terrorism.

As globalization forces the world to open the doors to neoliberalism and naked capitalism, some of the planet's more depressing realities have been thrust into our active consciousness: 50,000 people die every day of malnutrition, 1.2 billion live with less than one dollar a day, while forty-six percent of the world's population lives with less than two dollars a day.

There were probably some people living in the remote wilderness who did not hear of what happened on September Eleventh, but apart from these few, most everybody else in the world knows what happened. Indeed, although the rich know little about the poor, the majority of the world's poor knows how the rich live. They are, for instance, aware that the U.S. and the Western European nations spend more than $50 billion a year on alcohol, $17 billion on cosmetics, and an equal amount on pet food. How must this seem to someone who performs back-breaking work for two dollars a day?

The litany of statistics produces a never-ending paradox of contrasts. Infant mortality, for example, as an indicator of the quality of health care and general public health and sanitation, offers a frightening picture of the disparities between rich and poor. Whereas in the most developed countries, there are only 20 infant deaths for every 100,000 births, the number rises to 500 deaths for every 100,000 births in the less developed nations. If that statistic isn't shocking enough, one only has to look to Africa, where there are some countries in which the infant mortality rate reaches almost 1000 for every 100,000 births.

There are 1.2 billion people who have no access to proper drinking water and 1 billion with no decent living quarters. 840 million human beings suffer from malnutrition, of these, 200 million are children under the age of five. There are 880 million people who have no access to basic health services; 2 billion do not have the means to obtain necessary medication. This lack of basic health care causes serious epidemics in the developing world ranging from AIDS to tuberculosis to malaria. The diseases put children at greatest risk so that both the human and economic potential of these countries are minimized.

THE DARKEST SIDE OF GLOBALIZATION

GLOBALIZATION FUNCTIONS IN ALL directions. The U.S. and Western Europe cannot consider themselves isolated islands while simultaneously making their presence felt in every corner of the earth. The people occupying those far corners are starting to do whatever they can to get the West to notice them; indeed, this is the root of the development of the newest brand of terrorism, suicide terror. These organizations are not operating out of remote villages and exotic mountains. They work and flourish within middle class neighborhoods in the U.S., Germany, Spain, France, Italy, Sweden, England, etc. In fact, the officials of several Western countries were shocked at the number and array of countries mentioned in documents found by a London Times reporter in Kabul. For our own need to make sense out of the universe, we want to think that these terrorists should somehow be obvious to us, that they should stand out in some sinister way, and yet the members of terrorist groups usually appear to be absolutely normal. They are usually well-spoken (in several languages, no less), and they worship, work, and attend school like everyone else. Neoliberalism, so highly touted by many in the West, actually helps the new terrorists in their cause. Their new fangled mixture of guerilla warfare and organized crime makes the cities and society as a whole vulnerable. The world knows they are there, knows that they operate globally, but it can't single them out or stop them. Is this then the price of an unfair globalization?

seventeen:
"operation iraqui freedom"

More than fifty years ago, America won a war against
Fascism, which it followed up with a "Marshall Plan" and
"Nation-building," both a hand out and a hand up in a way
that made Americans welcome across the world. Today is the
D-Day for our generation. May our leaders have the wisdom
of their predecessors from the Greatest Generation.
— Thomas L. Friedman (2003, p. 8)

DAILY, SPORADIC BUT DEADLY shooting continues throughout Iraq: Baghdad, Basra, Fallujah. The general atmosphere that accompanied the second Gulf War did not allow for any type of official proclamation of victory or clear-cut end. This is not all that surprising as the end of a war often does not actually occur until many years after official proclamations and statements.

The war itself was a long time coming. Since September Eleventh, 2001, fear, suspicions, repeated warnings, and diplomatic blunders pointed inexorably to a repeat of the first Gulf War. This was, however, not to be an exact repeat, a bombing campaign followed by a fast and limited ground campaign with overwhelming international consensus. From the start, this new and virtually unilateral incursion into Iraq was labeled "The Twenty-First Century Fiasco," "another Bay of Pigs," and "a second Somalia" by critics and analysts. When the actual invasion began on March twentieth, 2003, a cloud of uncertainty loomed over the endeavor. The specter of another long and bloody conflict was raised as memories of the Vietnam War crept into the headlines and op-ed pages. Familiar questions were once again being asked by critics, most notably, how many coffins of killed U.S. soldiers would have to be paraded to change American public opinion, which had been so opposed to President Bush's crusade against Saddam Hussein.

Once again, television viewers were bombarded with constant news about the progress of the invasion. In fact, during late March and early April, practically the only thing being broadcast was the war in Iraq. But this coverage was different than that of previous conflicts. There was a new gimmick, reports that bordered on sensationalism which deceptively displayed the ultra-modern technology of current-day warfare. This gave the viewer the sensation of watching some kind of sanitized video game and lulled people into believing that a modern war could be won without devastating military or human losses.

This "war game" atmosphere was bolstered with an outrageous statement dating back to the Clinton Administration, but asserted anew, namely, "We will keep our fighting men and women out of harm's way" (cited in: Lukacs, 2003, p. 9).

As events unfolded, the television broadcasting was made to appear almost prophetic and magical. Various factors contributed to the style of media coverage in this war, including the appetite for sensationalism on the part of the American public and the lack of military experience or basic knowledge on the part of the broadcast media. The latter, especially, is a great disservice to the American people as well as to the entire world. As Ralph Peters sardonically pointed out, "Wouldn't it be lovely ... if just a few of those men and women preening for the cameras in their 'combat correspondent' get-ups would spend just a little less time in front of mirrors and just a bit more learning about war?" (2002, p. A10).

What they needed to learn and convey to their viewing public was the simple fact that war is not a game of any kind.

Thankfully, the young men and women, both American and British, who participated in this conflict as professional, trained military personnel, knew this already. Yes, they knew they had all the high-tech equipment at their disposal: powerful new generation Howitzers, updated Abrams M1A1 tanks, and the latest model armored vehicles. These coalition forces, fighting under separate American and British commands on different fronts, did their job with the utmost professionalism, simultaneously doing a grand job of silencing those who delight in any kind of setback to the Anglo-American coalition.

Nevertheless, it was a real war, one in which soldiers die, as the numbers indicate: one hundred and thirty-eight Americans and thirty-four British troops were killed. Four hundred and twenty-seven were wounded. Seven soldiers went missing during the fighting, but were later rescued. And thirteen war correspondents were killed doing their duty.

The number of fallen Iraqi soldiers is probably impossible to calculate, although it probably reaches into the thousands. The main problem is defining what constituted a "soldier" on the Iraqi side, as many fought out of uniform, and many were forced to fight. It is thus difficult to label casualties as either civilian or military. Mark Burgess, a researcher at the private Center for Defense Information in Washington D.C., affirmed this, asserting that "The war in Iraq presented unusually difficult problems in estimating the dead because few military units fought in an organized manner" (cited in: Broder, 2003, p. 3).

War is a repugnant, violent, cruel, and deadly business. War is not victory or defeat, but suffering and death. And no one should be fooled into thinking that the end of a war is marked by peace, because it is not. Rather, it is marked by what is known as a "post war" period.

Thus, even though the nightly bombing campaigns are over, and the majority of invading soldiers have been sent back to the U.S. and Britain, chaos, misery, and devastation are still the hallmarks of daily life in Iraq. The pain of the Iraqi people will last for years to come.

Washington and London may have presumed that they could "surgically" remove Saddam Hussein from power and leave the functioning civic structures intact. This, however, has not proven to be the case. The images of continuous smoke and flames over the cities of Baghdad and Basra, the terrified looks on the faces of the Iraqi civilians, the lifeless bodies of Iraqi men, women, and children on the debris-ridden streets, gave us only the slightest glimpse of the horror of war. Anarchy, danger, and fear continued to hamper efforts to deliver emergency relief such as food and medical supplies to treat the wounded and traumatized. Even weeks after the war, drinking water was not readily available in Baghdad or Basra. The fear of dysentery and cholera epidemics grew within a population already malnourished. The risk, of course, was greatest for the weakest members of the population, the elderly and the very young.

To exacerbate the fact that medicine and hospital supplies were already difficult to come by, at the end of the conflict, hospitals and health care centers were subject to looting. This left the population totally without medical care. Medicine, antibiotics, anesthetics, and painkillers were no longer available to treat the sick.

It was precisely this type of situation that Article 55 of the Fourth Geneva Convention meant to address. The article urges that:

To the fullest extent of the means available to it, the occupying power has the duty of insuring the food and medical supplies of the population; it should, in particular, bring in the necessary food stuffs, medical supplies and other articles, if the resources of the occupied territory are inadequate. (Cited in: Chelala, 2003, p. 8)

Humanitarian workers, generally coordinated under the auspices of the U.N., were not able to enter Iraq immediately, as the initial phase of the war took longer than expected. This prompted the leaders of various humanitarian organizations within the U.S. to complain to the Government for keeping them out of the plans for relief and reconstruction in Iraq. Only after Baghdad had fallen, over five weeks after the onset of the war, were humanitarian organizations able to enter the country, groups such as the Red Cross, Save the Children, UNICEF, the World Food Bank, and the World Health Organization.

Apart from the humanitarian crisis that confronted the victors, there was also the more mundane problem of establishing law and order. The chaos and anarchy unleashed by the fall of Saddam's regime spared nothing, not even the ancient archeological treasures of the Iraqi National Museum, which was pillaged by Iraqi marauders. Seven thousand years of historical artifacts dating back to the ancient kingdom of Mesopotamia, the cradle of civilization, were unceremoniously robbed or vandalized by a population at the breaking point. The occupying forces did little to stop the lawlessness. Defense Secretary Donald Rumsfeld was even quoted as saying, "Freedom is untidy and free people are free to commit mistakes and commit crimes" (cited in: Bringing safety..., 2003, p. 6). Apparently, Secretary Rumsfeld confused the looting, anarchy, and revenge for features of freedom, when, in fact, they were consequences of war.

These concerns of inadequate aid relief and the problem of establishing order in post-war Iraq would perhaps not be so compelling in the long run if political observers did not see a recurrent pattern of behavior by the Bush Administration. Paul Krugman, in an editorial entitled "The Bush Way: A Pattern of Conquest and Neglect," wrote, "We worry and continue to worry about what would follow, but there is a 'pattern' to the Bush Administration's way of doing business that does not bode well for the future, a 'pattern' of conquest followed by malign neglect" (2003, p. 6). The situation in Afghanistan, for example, after the U.S.'s overwhelming victory over the Taliban regime in 2001, has reverted back to its old ways. Power has once again landed in the hands of fundamentalist warlords whose influence is rooted in endless civil conflict supported by drug cartels buying the country's opium crop. To paraphrase the brother of the current President of Afghanistan, Hamid Karzai, the country is basically a rerun of the same movie as before, and nobody seems to care about disarming the warlords and their small armies or helping rebuild the infrastructure so desperately needed. Apparently, the last budget President Bush signed couldn't be stretched any farther to include Afghanistan.

Michael Kinsley, editor of the magazine *Slate*, put it bluntly: "Bush people are very good about breaking the rules and promises and after the victory, they leave the wreckage behind. I do hope to be proven wrong" (cited in: Krugman, 2003, p. 8). If the U.S. wishes to have any support for its ambitious "nation shaping" in the future, it must take seriously its duty to improve the present and create a hopeful future for Iraq.

eighteen:
an open letter to
president bush

DEAR PRESIDENT BUSH,

In a recent article by Bob Woodward (2002) you are quoted as saying, "The U.S. has to confront not only the strategic problems but the humanitarian issues as well" (p. 4).

Mr. Bush, the press, particularly the European press, has criticized, mocked, and bad-mouthed you since you left Austin, Texas in 1999 to campaign for the presidency.

Analysts and critics have given you names not worth mentioning here; they have compared you unfavorably with your predecessors to make you look like an odd, inferior fellow. The pundits have been joined by many political figures from the other side of the Atlantic, who have not behaved much more civilly to you, even though they should know better.

After you became a goldmine for comedians such as Jay Leno and David Letterman, people who heard your speeches and your acknowledgement of being an alcoholic and having other problems began to think that you are a normal human being. Perhaps Lou Goodman, dean at the American University in Washington said it best: "People feel that there is in the White House a type of fellow like them" (cited in: Valenzuela, 2001, p. 24). Even some of those who oppose your political viewpoints found you to be likeable enough. For example, Tim Schreiber, an engineering student, democrat, and critic of your desire to exploit the Alaskan oilfields, expressed his desire to have a beer with you, saying, "Mr. Bush seems to be nice" (cited in: Valenzuela, 2001, p. 23).

I am sure your advisors keep you informed to the utmost, Mr. President. But I think it is important that you hear how normal Americans view you and your actions. And it is important that you see how our allies abroad interpret what we do. So it was a shock to America's allies when, after having promised during the presidential campaign that you would be humble in your dealings with foreign affairs, you decided to bury the Kyoto Protocol soon after you got to the White House. This decision annoyed not only environmentalists but also many European leaders, for whom environmental issues are increasingly important. In fact, the French Minister for the Environment, Dominique Voyne remarked, "This is a scandal" (cited in: Yarnoz, 2001, p. 30).

This decision is especially grave since the U.S. is one of the biggest polluters in the world. Representatives from Greenpeace protested the refusal to join the Kyoto protocol, saying, "This is a slap in the face to the international community" (Yarnoz, 2001, p. 30).

In another area of policy, the cancellation of the ABM treaty and your intention to build the antimissile shield project triggered the French president, Jacques Chirac, to say, "It is an invitation for the proliferation of weapons" (Yarnoz, 2001, p. 30).

The twenty-year energy sources program announced by you raised the eyebrows of many. The Swedish minister for the Ecological Environment for United Europe, Margot Walltröm, went to Washington to talk personally with your staff, hoping to turn things around. Upon her return, however, her overwhelming impression from the meeting was one of disappointment.

The litany of issues and complaints is long, but let me finish the series with the statement made by Carlos Coelho, the Eurodeputy from Portugal: "Mr. Bush, during his presidential campaign, promised to be humble with foreign policy, but his actions show the opposite" (cited in: Yarnoz, 2001, p. 30).

This, however, was all before September Eleventh, 2001. That tragedy brought out a side of you that few ever expected to see, for you managed that event and its aftermath with both humility and firmness.

You understood that there is nothing, literally nothing, that justifies terrorism. Moved by uncompromising conviction, you committed yourself to the protection of your nation and its citizens when you made the fight against terrorism the highest objective of your administration (The presidency that began. . ., 2001, p. 6).

Mr. Bush, this war is not going to have a date of completion or a victory parade. It will be an ongoing struggle, but one which might be enhanced with the dose of medicine recently prescribed by a *New York Times* editorial: "The war against terror requires Washington to build and lead a broad coalition using diplomatic as well as military tools and hold it together for many years to come" (The message. . ., 2002, p. 6). This is a sentiment shared by a huge number of people, even though some of your advisors have advised you to the contrary, urging you to go it alone. Nobody on earth has doubts concerning your ability, power, and confidence. But you must remember that allies are necessary to guarantee peace and to assist transition governments in countries where the American armed forces would feel uncomfortable and would thus be less effective at maintaining order.

As for fighting terrorism, you seem to understand that negotiations and appeasement do not work. However, helping less fortunate countries develop the social structures that will strengthen their political and economic stability will alleviate hunger and despair, which are the trump cards of terrorist recruiters. Besides fighting terrorism actively and ameliorating poverty in countries which produce terrorists, however, there are still other problems that need addressing. These include global warming, proliferation of nuclear and biological weapons, and fighting the scourges of AIDS and malaria (America the aloof, 2002, p. 6). The responsibility of the only superpower is weighty, but America is well-equipped to shoulder that load.

Especially now that the American people, both Republicans and Democrats, showed their support for your political philosophy and handling of the issues by voting for Republican candidates in the last elections. The outcome was interpreted as a boost for you, the Commander in Chief. Still, you showed great restraint in your reaction to these victories, which was intelligent. But even though your party has gained control of both the House and the Senate, virtually guaranteeing easy passage of your political programs, the Democrats warn that you are presiding over "the weakest economic growth in fifty years" (Allen & Milbank, 2002, p. 3).

Indeed, the economy is shaky, seeming to rest on quick sand with no signs of solid ground in the near future. This problem cannot be overlooked, for to do so would be to risk the obvious reminder of what happened to your father ten years ago, when he lost his run for reelection, even after his meritorious victory in the Gulf War.

You should thus keep the economy in mind, Mr. President, and come down hard on white collar crime. As it is, your name is being connected far too often with the Enrons, Worldcoms, Adelphias, and other corporate institutions which have been found to be fraught with fraud and corruption. It doesn't matter that the wrong-doing started in the 1990s, before you ever became president. The fact is that as the deceit grew and could no longer be kept secret, the whole mess landed on the front lawn of the White House. And analysts feel that the U.S. economy is still "trying to get past the damage done by greedy executives" (Reforming..., 2002, p. 6).

Much newspaper ink has been dedicated to the way you protect some of the aforementioned executives, who have in many cases been your staunch political supporters. You are, as many columnists point out, "a man who believes strongly in loyalty" (Wondering..., 2002, p. 6). This is, of course, a noble quality, but many Americans, some who have lost their pensions or insurance benefits, feel that it is unfair that such executives continue on with their luxurious life-style. Where is justice? Where are the tough ethical stands which will give investors more confidence? As Alan Blinder (2002) remarks, "The markets are clamoring for decisive government action now" (p. 8).

But let us return to your top priority, fighting terrorism. Is the best answer to that threat the establishment of the TIPS (Terrorist Information and Prevention) program? It smacks of some Iron Curtain era spy story, encouraging us to observe and report on the movements of the postman, the garbage collector, and the gas meter reader. What is next? As Paul Kennedy (2002) from Yale University writes: "The U.S. is unable to live according to the ideals the country had defined: democracy, openness, respect for human rights and the commitment to keep the four freedoms" (p. 13). Mr. President, perhaps this is exaggerated, but we must be extremely careful not to forget the underlying spirit of our nation, otherwise, Kennedy's words will be more than just editorial comments.

While it is important to be careful and aware that the danger of terrorism is there, the alerts issued by the CIA and the FBI seem to compete with and be exacerbated by the news media. This creates a version of stimulus overload so that the majority of citizens start to ignore the alerts all together, while others become overly preoccupied, anxious, and almost paranoid. Jefferson's caveat that the price of freedom is eternal vigilance still rings true, but this vigilance should not be in exchange of America's mental health or its commitment to the four basic freedoms.

Mr. President, I find this issue quite paradoxical. You like to apply the law and abide by it, but the refusal to join the ICC (International Criminal Court) is "an act that the other nations perceive as a cavalier gesture of American unilateralism" (Denying global justice, 2002, p. 6). Some critics wrote that you did not want to sign the treaty to warn other countries that they should abandon their intentions of bringing Ariel Sharon to the ICC to answer for his actions against the Palestinians. Whether that was your motive or not, the fact is that the situation in Israel is untenable. In the words of Michael Wines (2002):

> If the international community does not act seriously to the arbitrariness and the challenges of the Sharon government, the Middle East region as a whole will become an area of instability and unrest whose dangerous results and consequences will tell on the whole world. (p. 8)

The arbitrariness of Sharon and the madness of the Palestinian terror groups are uncontainable and, unfortunately, feeding off each other. The result: innocent people crying for their loved ones who have been killed in the never-ending violence. Under your leadership, the U.S., must lead the way to a lasting solution, as difficult as this seems. Otherwise, the war on terror is just a bandage over a gaping wound.

Mr. President, in your first State of the Union address, you pointed the finger at what you called the "Axis of Evil Nations," namely North Korea, Iraq, and Iran. You labeled the regimes in power in these countries unworthy of trust. This statement caused many political leaders and analysts on the other side of the Atlantic to criticize you and there is no sign that they are ready to recant that criticism. Even after Kim, the North Korean dictator, acknowledged in front of his country's Communist Politburo that North Korea possesses nuclear weapons, nobody has the courage to take back the harsh words they aimed at you. That Iran has nuclear projects on the table is also well-known, as the Russians have actually been asked to stop assisting that country with said projects. And Iraq, of course, has finally been pressured enough to allow the U.N. weapons inspectors back into the country; it remains to be seen if the U.N. will let itself be hoodwinked yet another time by Saddam Hussein.

Do not be discouraged by your European critics; they feel that it is their job to act as a robust, but democratic opposition. In fact, as one editorial put it, "Like some past arguments between the allies, this one will be worth it if it succeeds in creating a new and solid front of resistance to a common enemy, in this case antidemocratic regimes that pursue nuclear and biological weapons" (Cross talk..., 2002, p. 8).

President Bush, I have heard and read that you are a compassionate person. It is with this in mind that I wish to point out to you the root of the problems of terrorism, brutality and war. As we fight the dictators and antidemocratic regimes of the "evil nations," we must not forget the millions of people desperate with hunger and poverty, many facing imminent starvation and death, especially in the impoverished African nations which have been subjected to severe drought conditions for the last ten years. I wish to remind you of the words that you yourself said not long ago:

> We fight against poverty because hope is an answer to terrorism. We fight against poverty because opportunity is a fundamental right and human dignity. We fight against poverty because faith requires it and conscience demands it. (Aid to poor, 2002, p. 1)

President Bush, the world is waiting for your statement to become reality.

WHILE THE WORLD WAS WAITING, you toppled Saddam's regime and captured the dictator himself. Mr. President, the declaration on May the first, of the end of the conventional war in Iraq, gave birth to an unconventional war.

You have been quoted as saying, "There are some who feel like the conditions are such that they can attack the U.S. there. My answer is, bring them in. We got the force necessary to deal with the security issue" [Editorial letter 2003, p. A20]. Saddam's followers, Mr. President, do not need to be incited to kill.

The American, English, and Allied soldiers are fighting three armies. The first, unhappy Iraqi who are faithful followers of Saddam Hussein; the second army is the "culture," the Iraqi way of life – phenomenon engraved in the Iraqi psyche for several decades in spite of the torture, oppression, and lack of freedom; and the third army is made of hordes of Islamic volunteers from all over the world who feel religiously obligated to fight against infidels who occupied Iraq. "If you read the Koran closely, it says you must fight against the infidels who occupy your country. This is clear. There is no choice. We are not paid money; we are guests of Iraqis staying in their homes," said a young Muslim fighter from Jordan [Walt, Vivienne, 2003, p. A9].

Mr. President, arms do not change a "culture," a way of life; food, water, electricity, jobs, education, better living conditions and "TIME" will do it.

You have been calling on the U.N. to assist with the Iraq situation. Your call is encountering the usual resistance from the European superpowers – Germany, France and Russia. Germany and France need the flow of Iraqi oil, as they had with Saddam Hussein, and Russia wants to recover the billions invested in Iraq during the Saddam regime.

The "Road Map" program for the Middle East did not work in spite of your efforts. The people from both camps do not want peace, it seems. Mr. Arafat's power was underestimated and there was no office or room for Mr. Abbas.

Mr. President, you are holding the support of many American people. Nevertheless, besides fighting terrorism and keeping the security meter on a high alert mode, the economy needs to get stronger. It carries a heavy load of unemployment.

The recalling of September Eleventh has not stopped terror attacks or the threat of new ones by the bin Laddens and the al Qaedas against the U.S. The Middle East, Afaghanastan and Iraq will not go away. Unfortunately, the death of U.S. soldiers will rise, and the price of these wars will soar. These issues are complicated and sensitive no matter what, but particularly in your drive to be re-elected to the Presidency for a second term.

Mr. President, America and the world are anxiously waiting for constructive resolutions.

epilogue

It is difficult for any human being to imagine the total and suicidal craziness, but that is what we are heading to if we don't turn around the present situation.
— Gabriel Jackson (2001, A propósito... , p. 19)

A S APOCALYPTIC AS THE EVENTS of September Eleventh may have seemed, many observers believe that we have witnessed just the beginning of what terrorists have in store. Social science scholars predict that the crash against the World Trade Center, which burst into flames due to the 300 tons of fuel on board and subsequently collapsed, killing 3000 innocent people, will more than likely be outdone by an even larger catastrophe; the scenario that seems most plausible is the explosion of a weapon of mass destruction in a major city.

If they choose to reflect on the situation at hand, world leaders should be very concerned with what might happen in the next few years when the "nuclear club" proliferates, either through espionage or economic interests, expanding its membership from seven nations to thirty or forty, plus a handful of international mafia and terrorist organizations that manage to obtain or produce nuclear, chemical, and biological weapons.

It may sound alarmist, but the possibility that nuclear arms may fall into the hands of radical, fundamentalist governments that do not make a clear distinction between terror and usefulness is a real one. The hostilities between India and Pakistan over Kashmir raise the specter of a nuclear war on the subcontinent. Perhaps that seems too distant to concern the West, but rest assured that the loss of life would be on a scale such as the world has never seen.

Should we be concerned? The President of Pakistan, Pervez Musharraf, stated in an interview with CNN that, "I believe that neither side is so irresponsible as to go to that extreme" (cited in: Musharraf descuenta..., 2002, p. 12). While that may allay the fears of some in the West, it is important to keep in mind that Pakistan's radical Muslims believe and openly assert that the country's nuclear weapons should be part of the Jihad's arsenal. These same people have proven recently that they are willing to act upon their beliefs.

Saddam Hussein, the autocratic dictator of Iraq, had been developing chemical and biological weapons for many years. He was known to have a big appetite for nuclear weapons as well. Over the years he demonstrated again and again that he would put his money where his mouth was, surviving one war against the U.S. and succumbing in a second. In between he tortured thousands of his countrymen, even using chemical weapons in his own country to kill thousands of unarmed citizens of the Kurdish minority.

As mentioned above, Hussein wantonly flaunted U.N. sanctions imposed on Iraq in 1991 after the Gulf War by refusing to allow U.N. arms inspectors into the country. He maintained this stance from 1998 until 2003; indeed, it was only when the U.S. became intent on going to war that Hussein wrote to U.N. General Secretary Kofi Annan and promised to let the inspectors back in.

This was a man that was reported by The Washington Post to have continued his arms program to develop weapons of mass destruction, even in the face of international sanctions. He used chemical weapons on his own population. He only offered to cooperate after extreme pressure had been placed on him. He was not to be trusted and now he is gone.

Perhaps we are merely being paranoid. Just how real is the nuclear threat? It is serious enough that the International Atomic Energy Agency (IAEA) has outlined several possible scenarios concerning nuclear terrorism. They include the following:

• The threat of scientists going over to "the other side" or selling nuclear technology to terrorists or governments straining at the bit to obtain nuclear weapons. This is actually more likely than the threat of a terrorist organization stealing an atomic weapon.

• The threat of an attack on a nuclear power plant to trigger an explosion. Such a blast would trigger uncontrollable emissions of radioactivity into the surrounding areas, causing death and devastation.

• The threat of terrorists actually being able to deliver and detonate an atomic bomb, given that they could obtain access to one, is not excessively high, but such groups have shown great resourcefulness, so such a scheme cannot be ruled out.

• The threat of a terrorist organization fabricating a "dirty bomb" involving the explosion of radioactive material via conventional explosives. This is another very real possibility.

The fact is, it is not difficult to produce such weapons. Ulrich Beck (2001), a professor of social science at the University of Munich in Germany recently wrote an essay entitled "The Silence of Words," in which he describes how almost anyone could make a biological-atomic bomb on a small scale with minimal resources. The artifact would be capable of producing a genetic plague with a more or less prolonged period of incubation to threaten a city. As horrific as this sounds, it is only one example among the many detailed by Beck. When asked about the consequences of such an attack, Steven Koonin, a physicist and national security expert who is currently the provost of the California Institute of Technology, commented, "I think we'd be in real trouble… you wouldn't want to go back to old Manhatten" (cited in: Glanz & Revkin, 2001, p 3). Needless to say, the consequences of a dirty bomb explosion would be psychologically devastating, not to mention costly. It would cause extensive contamination that would in all likelihood never completely dissipate, as well as lead to human suffering and death.

Just how does a modern democracy deal with such threats? Donald Rumsfeld, Secretary of Defense, commented on this issue one year after the September eleventh attacks:

> We must be prepared, the future will demand new ways of thinking and establishing forces and instruments that could be adapted quickly to new challenges of unexpected circumstances. The capability to adapt will be fundamental in a world defined by surprise and uncertainty. (Plate, 2002, p. 6)

This is the current way of thinking among U.S. government officials; indeed, senior administration officials are now warning that "attempts by terrorists to attack the U.S. with a weapon of mass destruction are all but inevitable" (Safeguarding…, 2002, p. 8).

As the famous Peruvian author Mario Vargas Llosa (2001) intimated after the September Eleventh attacks, the thought that a band of crazed, well-funded fundamentalists could detonate an atomic artifact in the middle of Fifth Avenue, Piccadilly Circus, or the Champs Elysées, poisoning the air, water, or food supply of a major city or infesting it with a killer bacteria has ceased to be the stuff of Hollywood movies or computer games. It has been transformed to a menacing reality of our time.

references

(All translations are by the author.)

1953 Frustrated by Korean War. (2003, January 10). *International Herald Tribune*,
    p. 10.

A common language to punish terrorism. (2001, December 7). *El País*, p. 18.

Abdelkarium, R.Z. (2001, September 14). United in Pain and Anger. *El País*,
    international sec., p. 24.

Aid to poor linked to anti-terror efforts. (2002, March 23). *International Herald
    Tribune*, p. 1.

Allen, M. & Milbank, D. (2002, October 16). Bush shifts blame on economy.
    International Herald Tribune, p. 3.

Allen, W. (2001, Sept 22). Woody Allen. *El País*, p. 22.

America the aloof. [Editorial]. (2002, July 14). *International Herald Tribune*, p. 6.

Aznarez, J.J. (2002, August 29). The U.S. does not appreciate enough our condition
    as associates. *El País*, international sec., 6.

Barton, G. (2001, December 21). From third tier to top gear. *International Herald
    Tribune*, p. 3.

Beck, U. (2001, December 16). El silencio de las palabras [The silence of words].
    [Editorial]. *El País*, p. 15.

Becker, E. & Dao, J. (2002, February 21). Speaking of diplomacy: Bush will
    globalized the message. *International Herald Tribune*, p 3.

Bergen, P.L. (2001, November 5). Holy War. *Financial Times*, p. 7.

Bergsten, F. (2002, May 2). America and Europe Together. *International Herald Tribune*, p. 8.

Blinder, A. (2002, July 22). A time for government action. *International Herald Tribune*, p. 8.

Bringing safety to the streets. (2003, April 15). [Editorial]. *International Herald Tribune*, p. 6.

Broder, J.M. (2003, April 11). Effort to tally Iraqi deaths is complicated by the chaos of war. *International Herald Tribune*, p. 3.

Bumiller, E. & Sanger, D.E. (2002, January 2). For Bush, tests on home front. *International Herald Tribune*, p 4.

Carlin, J. (2001, September 16). End of an era. *El País*, p. 13.

Carlin, J. (2001, December 30). Viaje a la América herida. *El País Semanal*, p. 50.

Chelala, C. (2003, April 16). Act fast to save Iraqi children. *International Herald Tribune*, p. 8.

Chomski, N. (2001, November 1). The new war against terror. *Le Monde Diplomatique*, p. 3.

Cross talk among the allies. [Editorial]. (2002, February 12). *International Herald Tribune*, p. 8.

Davis, W. (2002, July 6-7). The root of disaffection: For a global declaration of interdependence. *International Herald Tribune*, p. 8.

De Rituerto, R. (2001, September 13). A secret investigation detected serious failures in airports. *El País*, international sec., p. 9.

Denying global justice. [Editorial]. (2002, May 20). *International Herald Tribune*, p. 6.

Dorfman, A. (2001, September 17). The other September eleventh. [Editorial]. *El País*, p. 30.

Dorsey, J.M. (2001, November 5). Islamic scholars develop definition for terrorism. *Wall Street Journal* (European Ed.), p. 4.

Dwyer, J. (2002, September 11). Una cinta rescata las voces de los bomberos muertos. *El País*, p. 18.

Dwyer, J. et al. (2002, May 27). Final moments of World Trade Center will never be lost. *International Herald Tribune*, p. 2.

Eggen, D. & Dobbs, M. (2002, January 15). Down but not out: Al Qaeda danger persists. *International Herald Tribune*, pp. 1, 14.

Elorza, A. & Elorza, A. (2001, September 27). The Allah Puritans. *El País*, international sec., p. 21.

Erlanger, S. (2002, February 25). As U.S. goes it alone.... . *International Herald Tribune*, p. 17.

Fresneda, C. (2003, March 30). La 'paz virtual se cultiva en internet. *El Mundo*, p. 20.

Friedman, T.L. (2002, February 21). Running on empty. *International Herald Tribune*, p. 9.

_____. (2003, March 20). Cowboys, posses and black hats. *International Herald Tribune*, p. 8.

Fuller, T. (2002, February 5). Investigators shift their focus to 'free-lance' terrorists. *International Herald Tribune*, p. 4.

Gardels, N. (2002, March 14). Robert McNamara, ex secretario de defensa. *El País*, p. 4.

Garton Ash, T. (2001, September 26). We do not know how a Muslim terrorist thinks yet. *El País*, international sec., p. 21.

Gaztelu, J.P. (2002, October 20). The return of Al Qaeda. *El País*, p. 4.

Glanz, J. & Revkin, A.. (2001, November 5). Materials at hand in U.S. to make a 'dirty' bomb. *International Herald Tribune*, pp 3-4.

Goldberg, J. (2001, September 16). La universidad del fanatismo. *El País*, p. 7.

Gonzalez, E. (2001, September 13). Bush: it has been an act of war. *El País*, international sec., p. 2.

_____. (2002, September 25). Gore vuelve a la escena política. *El País*, p. 4.

_____. (2003, January 30). Bush prepara a los EE.UU. para la guerra en Iraq. *El País*, p. 2.

_____. (2003, March 9). La hora del presidente. *El País*, p. 2.

Gordon, M.R. (2003, January 28). Bush preemption doctrine: will Iraq be the first test? *International Herald Tribune*, p. 1.

Gordon, N. (2002, September 11). Fear. *El Mundo*, p. 6.

Hoagland, J. (2002, February 8). The U.S. military colossus will be right to focus on Saddam. *International Herald Tribune*, p. 1.

Hoffman, B. (2002, September 11). Is a bigger attack possible? *El Mundo*, p. 20.

Ignatius, D. (2001, December 20). A changed world. *International Herald Tribune*, p. 6.

Jackson, G. (2001, November 23). A propósito de las armas de destrucción masiva. *El País*, international sec., p. 19.

_____. (2002, May 29). Los verdaderos objetivos de Bush. *El País*, p. 13.

Johnston, A. (2001, December 20). Disparities of wealth are seen as fuel for terrorism. *International Herald Tribune*, p. 6.

Kahn, J. (2002, January 2). For poor Muslims an economic alternative to terrorism. *International Herald Tribune*, p. 13.

Kapuscinski, R. (2002, February 24). Un mundo, dos civilizaciones. *El País*, p. 18.

_____. (2002, September 29). La globalización del mal. *El País*, p. 9.

Kennedy, P. (2002, March 7). Como ven otros a los EE.UU. tiene importancia. *El País*, international sec., pp. 11,14.

———. (2002, October 8). Bush history lesson. *El País*, p. 14.

Krugman, P. (2003, April 13). The Bush way. *International Herald Tribune*, p. 6.

Lamo de Espinosa, E. (2001, October 26). Ciudadanos de los Estados Unidos. *El País*, p. 25.

Lefort, C. (2001, December 9). Bin Laden and his people will mark the process of globalization. *El País Semanal*, p. 6.

Leow, R. (2002, February 15). How can globalization become o.k. for all? *International Herald Tribune*, p. 9.

Lloris, M. (2001, November, 30) Los EE.UU. y nosotros. *El País*, p. 2.

López Perona, A. (2001). Los Talibán. *Política Exterior*, 15 (84), p. 79.

Lukacs, J. (2003, April 16). Meanwhile. *International Herald Tribune*, p. 9.

Mallaby, S. (2003, February 15). The wizard of Afghanistan. *International Herald Tribune*, p. 8.

Malley, R. (2003, March 7). Bush Irrational Rational. *International Herald Tribune*, p. 8.

Marin, M. (2001, September 15). Los niños no entienden. *El País*, international sec., p. 14.

Marozzi, J. (2001, September 27). With God on their board. *Financial Times*, p. 5.

Middle East confusion. [Editorial.] (2002, July 5). *International Herald Tribune*, p. 6.

Musharraf descuenta la opción nuclear (2002, June 2). *El País*, international sec., p. 12.

Naim, M. (2002, September 6). Six surprises. *El País*, international sec., p. 6.

Nuclear posturing. [Editorial.] (2002, March 15). *Wall Street Journal* (European ed.), p. 5.

O'Neil, P. (2001, November 15). U.S. makes progress on financial front. *Wall Street Journal* (European ed.), p. 3.

Ortega, A. (2001, December 17). Return to unilateralism. *El País*, international sec., p. 4.

Pervez Musharraf, presidente de Pakistán. (2002, April 9). *El País*, p. 6.

Peters, R. (2002, March 6). In war, soldiers die. [Editorial]. *Wall Street Journal* (European Ed.), p. A10.

Petersen, J. (2001, December 26). In the Mid-east, no security without negotiation. [Editorial.] *International Herald Tribune*, p. 6.

Pfaff, W. (2001, November 1). A precarious balance. *International Herald Tribune*, p. 3.

_____. (2002, January 10). The politics of terrorism. *International Herald Tribune*, p. 8.

_____. (2003, March 20). Diplomatic blunders led to war. *International Herald Tribune*, p. 8.

Pincus, W. (2002, February 22). And now the fine print on nuclear arms. *International Herald Tribune*, p. 3.

Piquer, I. (2002, August 26). Baker joins the critics. *El País*, international sec., p. 3.

Plate, T. (2002, September 3). September eleventh: a year after. *El País*, international sec., p. 6.

Prados, L. (2002, May 10). Más política, menos bombas. *El País*, p. 12.

Ramonet, I. (2002, September, 4). Power without limits. *El País*, international sec., p. 6.

Reforming capitalism. [Editorial]. (2002, July 27). *International Herald Tribune*, p. 6.

Richburg, K.B. (2001, May 2). Bush to get sympathetic ear. *International Herald Tribune*, p. 17.

Safeguarding Soviet arms. (2002, July 27-28). [Editorial]. *International Herald Tribune*, p. 8.

Sahagun, F. (2002, September 11). Claves para una nueva era. *El Mundo*, p. 19.

San Francisco Chronicle. (July 4, 2003). editorial letter. p. A20.

Saramago, J. (2002, February 6). Este mundo de la injusticia globalizada. [Editorial]. *El País*, p. 13.

Sennott, C.M. (2002, February 2). Financial regulators seize momentum. *International Herald Tribune*, p. 11.

Sipress, A. & Slevin, P. (2001, December 22/23). Powell warns of applying the Afghan model to Iraq. *International Herald Tribune*, p. 1.

Sounders, F.S. (2001, November 28). La CIA y la sociedad abierta. *El País*, p. 5.

Steiger, P. (2001, December 17). Military conquers myths in Afghan war. *Wall Street Journal* (European Ed.), p. 4.

Taylor, E. (2001, November 8). *Wall Street Journal* (European ed.), p. 2.

Tertsch, H. (2002, August 30). El Atlántico se ensancha. *El País*, international sec., p. 3.

Thatcher, M. (2002, February 8). Go ahead, make the world safer. *International Herald Tribune*, p. 8.

The message in Bali. [Editorial]. (2002, October 16). *International Herald Tribune*, p. 6.

The presidency that began Tuesday. [Editorial]. (2001, September 15). *Washington Post*, p. 6.

The U.S. information services were put on the stage by the terrorists. (2001, September 12). *El País*, international sec., p. 4.

Usborne, D. (2002, November 9). The day the world turned on Iraq. *The Independent*, p. 1.

Valenzuela, J. (2001, June 10). Porque los Americanos quieren a Bush. *El País Semanal*, p. 24.

_____. (2001, September 14). The enemy in the shadows. *El País*, international sec., p. 5.

Vargas Llosa, M. (2001, November 25). Novelista en Nueva York. *El País*, p. 17.

Vendrel, F. (2001, December 30). U.N. envoy to Afghanistan. *El País Semanal*, p. 22.

Verdu, V. (2003, February 23). La opinión pública como superpotencia. *El País*, 'Tendencias', p. 8.

Walt, Vivienne. (Nov. 28, 2003). Foreigners in Iraq say Koran Requires Fighting U.S., *San Francisco Chronicle*. p. A9.

Washington, P.G. (2001, October 4). The U.S. is being prepared against a bacteriological attack. *El País*, p. 11.

Weisel, E. (2002, September 11). We can't give up. *El Mundo*, p. 15.

Wines, M. (2002, April 20). [Editorial]. *International Herald Tribune*, p. 8.

Wondering about Bush. [Editorial]. (2002, July 22). *International Herald Tribune*, p. 6.

Woodward, B. (2002, November 20). Somos lideres y un líder debe tener la facultad de actuar. *El País*, p. 4.

Yarnoz, C. (2001, June 10). Porque los Europeos no quieren a Bus. *El País Semanal*, pp. 28-30.

_____. (2002, February 9). The E.U. condemns Bush policy. *El País*, international sec., p. 5.

_____. (2002, September 6). Europe resists aggressive Washington. *El País*, international sec., p. 4.

works consulted

Al Shariati. (1979). *The Sociality of Islam*. Berkeley: Berkeley Univ. Press.

Schmid, A.P. & Crelisten. (1993). *Western Response to Terrorism*. London: Frank Cass.

Negri, A. & Harot, M. (2000) *Empire*. Cambridge, MA: Harvard Univ. Press.

Archer, C. (2000). *The European Union: Structure and Process*. New York: Continuum.

Armstrong, K. (2000). *The Battle for God: Fundamentalism in Judaism, Christianity and Islam*. London, New York:.

Creshaw, M. (1995). *Terrorism in Context*. University Park, PA: Penn State Univ. Press.

David, J. M. (1997). *Between Jihad and Salam: Profiles in Islam*. New York:.

Riches, D. (1986). *Anthropology of Violence*.: Blackwell.

Dehouse, R. (1998). *The European Court of Justice*. Basingstoke, U.K.:Palgrave.

Emmanuel, T. (2002). *A Press L'Empire*.: Gallimard.

Nadelmann, E. (1993). *Cops Across Borders: The Internationalism of U.S. Criminal Law Enforcement*. University Park, PA: Penn State Univ. Press.

Stephen, G. & Bache, I. (2001). *Politics in the European Union*. Oxford: Oxford Univ. Press.

Halliday, F. (1996). *Islam and the Myth of Confrontation: Religion and Politics in the Middle East*. London, New York: .

Hoffman, B. (1998). *Inside Terrorism*. London: Indigo.

Hughes, R. (1993). *The Culture of Complaint.* New York: Oxford Univ. Press.

Huntington, S. (1968). *Political Order in Changing Societies.* New Haven, CT: Yale Univ. Press.

Hutchinson, R. (2001). *Sometime Lofty Towers.* San Francisco: Browntrout.

Nelson-Pall-Meyer, J. (1997). *School of Assassins: The Case for Closing the School of America and for Fundamentally Changing U.S. Foreign Policy.* Maryknoll, NY: Orbis.

Kagan, D. (1995). *On the Origin of War for the Preservation of Peace.* New York: Doubleday.

King, M.L.K. (1958) *Stride Towards Freedom: The Montgomery Story.* New York: Harper & Row.

Kissinger, H. (1999). *Diplomacy.* New York: Simon & Schuster.

Landes, D. (1998). *The Wealth and Poverty of Nations.* New York: Norton.

Laquer, W. (2001). *"The Changing Face of Terror."* How Did It Happen? New York: Foreign Affairs Reports.

Michel, L., Bernstein, J., & Schmitt, J. (1999). *The State of Working America: 1998-99.* Ithaca, NY: IRL Press.

Ortega y Gasset. (1985). *The Revolt of the Masses.* Indiana: Univ. of Notre Dame Press.

Ralph, P. (1999). *Fighting for the Future: Will America Triumph?* Mechanicsburg, PA: Stackpole.

Peterson, J. & Bomberg, E. (1999). *Decision Making in the European Union.* Basingstoke, U.K.: Palgrave.

Kagan, R. (1998, summer). *"The benevolent empire."* Foreign Policy, pp..

Schlesinger, A.M. (1986). *The Cycles of American History.* Boston, MA: Houghton Mifflin.

Schulz, N. et al. (1999). *Fear Itself.* Indiana: Purdue Univ. Press.

The Grand Chessboard: *American Primacy and its Geostrategic Imperatives.* (1997). : Basic Books.

Voll, J. (1982). *Islam: Continuity and Change in the Modern World.* Boulder, CO: .

Warleigh, A. (2002). *Understanding European Institutions.* London: Routledge

White, E.B. (1949). *Here is New York.* New York: Harper and Bros.

Whitman, R.G. (1998). *From Civilian Power to Super Power? The International Identity of the European Union.* New York: St. Martin's.

Wood, D. & Birol, Y. (2002). *The Emerging European Union.* London: Longman.